Necessary Spaces

Exploring the Richness of African American Childhood in the South

A volume in
Landscapes of Education
Ming Fang He and William Schubert, *Series Editors*

Necessary Spaces

*Exploring the Richness of African
American Childhood in the South*

Saundra Murray Nettles

University of Illinois at Urbana–Champaign

INFORMATION AGE PUBLISHING, INC.
Charlotte, NC • www.infoagepub.com

Library of Congress Cataloging-in-Publication Data

A CIP record for this book is available from the Library of Congress
http://www.loc.gov

ISBN: 978-1-62396-331-6 (Paperback)
        978-1-62396-332-3 (Hardcover)
        978-1-62396-333-0 (ebook)

Contents

List of Figures

Series Foreword

Landscapes of Education

William H. Schubert & Ming Fang He

In this book series, we explore panoramic landscapes of education. We invite a wide array of authors from diverse theoretical traditions and geographical locations around the world to ponder deeply and critically undulating and evolving contours of educational experience. We perceive contours of educational experience as landscapes that cultivate and are cultivated by who we were and how we become who we are as individuals and as humanity (Nussbaum, 1997). We engage with complex hills and rift valleys, rocky roads and serene pathways, war-torn terrains and flowering gardens, towering trees and wuthering grasses, jagged cliffs and unyielding rocks, flowing rivers and uneven oceans evolving with flows of life that shape our perspectives, modify our ideas, and forge our actions. Building upon John Dewey's (1916) *democratic conception of education* and William Schubert's (2009) *ideals of love, justice, and education*, we perceive landscapes of education not only as schools but also as *gathering places* (Dewey, 1933) for humans to pursue worthwhile living. We honor the poetics of landscapes of education flourishing with divergence, convergence, diversity, and complexity of experience.

We look for authors who can move in new directions. We open dialogue on educational issues and situations of shared concerns. We create a space

Necessary Spaces, pages ix–xvi
Copyright © 2013 by Information Age Publishing
All rights of reproduction in any form reserved.

for educational workers such as public intellectuals, scholars, artists, and practitioners to engage in inquiries into education drawn from multiple perspectives such as art, music, language, literature, philosophy, history, social sciences, and professional studies. We welcome cross-disciplinary, interdisciplinary, transdisciplinary, and counterdisciplinary work. We look for possibilities that are fresh and poetic, nuanced and novelistic, theoretical and practical, personal and political, imaginative and improvisational.

We expand parameters of educational inquiry substantively and methodologically. Substantively, books in this series explore multifarious landscapes wherever education occurs. Such explorations provocatively portray education in schools, workplaces, nonschool settings, and relationships. Methodologically, we encourage diverse forms of inquiry drawing on a wide array of research traditions, approaches, methods, and techniques such as ethnomethodology, phenomenology, hermeneutics, feminism, rhizomatics, deconstructionism, grounded theory, case studies, survey studies, interviews, participant observation, action research, teacher research, activist feminist inquiry, self-study, life history, teacher lore, autobiography, biography, memoir, documentary studies, art-based inquiry, ethnography/critical ethnography, autoethnography, participatory inquiry, narrative inquiry, fiction, cross-cultural and multicultural narrative inquiry, psychoanalysis, queer inquiry, and personal~passionate~participatory inquiry.

We also feature works that amplify the educational value of mass media such as movies, DVDs, television, the Internet, comics, news comedy, cell phones, MySpace and Facebook, videos, video games, computers, and the World Wide Web. We hope to explore how we learn through such electronic frontiers in vastly new ways with little tutelage. We hope to encourage creative improvising, problem posing, critical inquiring, and joyful learning illuminated in these new ways of learning through electronic frontiers that are often suppressed and repressed in schooling. We hope to acknowledge the power of human beings to learn without lesson plans, manuals, worksheets, standardized tests, acquisitive rewards, or external standards.

We encourage expansions that move beyond Western orthodoxies to embrace landscapes from the Eastern (Asian), Southern (African and Latin American), and Oceanic (islandic) worlds. We especially want to see renditions move into *third spaces* (Gutiérrez, Rymes, & Larson, 1995) and *in-between* (He, 2003, 2010) that push boundaries, shift borders, dissolve barriers, and thrive upon contradictions of life. It is our intention that the works featured in this series reveal more of the worldwide landscapes of cultures, ideas, and practices that transgress dominant Western ideologies and their corporate and colonizing legacies. These works have potential in developing transcendent theories of decolonization (e.g., Tuhiwai Smith,

1999/2005), advocating the liberty of indigenous language, cultural rights, and intellectualism (e.g., Grande, 2004), shattering *monocultures of the mind* (Shiva, 1993), overcoming perils of globalization, and inventing a better human condition for all.

We also highlight activist and social justice-oriented research (e.g., Ayers, Quinn, & Stovall, 2009) and personal~passionate~participatory inquiry (e.g., He & Phillion, 2008) that engage participation of all citizens, encourage respect, innovation, interaction, cohesion, justice, and peace, and promote cultural, linguistic, intellectual, and ecological diversity and complexity. We celebrate postcolonial feminist work (e.g., Minh-ha, 1989; Mohanty, 2003/2005; Narayan, 1997) that explores migration, slavery, suppression, resistance, representation, difference, race, gender, place, and responses to influential discourses of racism, sexism, classism, and colonialism. We also feature ecofeminist inquiry that explores the intersectionality of repatriarchal historical analysis, spirituality, racism, classism, imperialism, heterosexism, ageism, ableism, anthropocentrism, speciesism, and other forms of oppression (Mies & Shiva, 1993).

Books in this series focus on the what, why, how, when, where, and for whom of relationships, interactions, and transactions that transform human beings to different levels of awareness to build communities and public spaces with shared interests and common goals to strive for equitable, just, and invigorating human conditions. We seek explorations of the educational aspects of relationships (e.g., family, friendship), international, transnational, or intercultural understanding (e.g., exile, diaspora, displacement, indigenous knowledge), and circumstances of living (e.g., poverty, racism, alienation, war, colonization, oppression, and globalization). We want to see how languages, literacies, communities, homes, and families shape images of life's *mysteries and events* (Ulich, 1955), such as love, tradition, birth, death, success or failure, hopes of salvation, or immortality. These educational dimensions of life dynamically influence and are influenced by life in and out of schools (Schubert, 2010) and in-between (He, 2003, 2010). Through engaging such pursuits, this book series illuminates how human beings improvise lives (Bateson, 1989) and commitments in diverse, complicated, and often contested landscapes of education.

Unlike more definitively crafted book series that explicate inclusions and exclusions with ease and precision, our invitations continuously expand. The depths and breadths of landscapes where we live surpass everyday gaze and complicate static analysis. We showcase books that bring a sense of wonder and surprise, make the strange familiar and the familiar strange, and evoke what we do not expect. We do not narrow or define the topics of this series. Rather, we open doors to new perspectives, diverse paradigms, and creative possibilities. We invite authors to surprise us with their insightful ideas of what has been, what is, and what might be. In this volume,

> Saundra Murray Nettles takes the reader on a journey into neighborhood networks of learning at different times and places. Using autobiographical accounts, Nettles discusses the informal instructional practices of community "coaches" from the perspective of African American adults who look back on their childhood learning experiences in homes, libraries, city blocks, schools, churches, places of business, and nature. These eyewitness accounts reveal "necessary spaces," the metaphor Nettles uses to describe seven recurring experiences that converge with contemporary notions of optimal Black child development: connection, exploration, design, empowerment, resistance, renewal, and practice. Nettles weaves the personal stories with social scientific theory and research and practical accounts of community-based initiatives to illuminate how local communities contributed human, built, and natural resources to support children's achievement in schools. The inquiry offers a timely and accessible perspective on how community involvement for children can be developed utilizing the grassroots efforts of parents, children, and other neighborhood residents; expertise from personnel in schools, informal institutions (such as libraries and museums); and other sectors interested in disparities in education, health, and the quality of physical settings. Grounded in the environmental memories of African American childhood, *Necessary Spaces* offers a culturally relevant view of civic participation and sustainable community development at the local level. Educational researchers and policymakers, preservice and in-service teachers, and people who plan for and work with children and youth in neighborhoods will find this book an engaging look at possibilities for the social organization of educational resources. Qualitative researchers will find a model for writing personal scholarly essays that use the personal to inform larger issues of policy and practice. In *Necessary Spaces*, local citizens in neighborhoods across the United States will find stories that resonate with their own experiences, stimulate their recollections, and inform and inspire their continuing efforts to create brighter futures for children and communities (Backcover).

This book is a continuation of dialogue on curriculum of the South with a particular focus on the power of counternarrative as a means to contest traditional ways of engaging in and interpreting curriculum research and affirm the significance of autobiographical "eyewitness accounts" as a form of liberatory or radical democratic curriculum practice. The counternarratives of contested race, gender, class, power, sexuality, and place are exemplified in *Narrative of the Life of Frederick Douglass* (Douglass, 1845/2004), *Incidents in the Life of a Slave Girl* (Jacobs, 1861/2001), *Borderlands: La Frontera* (Anzuldua, 1987), *A Voice from the South* (Cooper, 1988), *Woman, Native, Other: Writing Postcoloniality and Feminism* (Minh-Ha, 1989),

Making Face, Making Soul: Creative and Critical Perspectives by Women of Color (Anzaldua, 1990), *Faces at the Bottom of the Well: The Permanence of Racism* (Bell, 1992), *Savage Inequalities: Children in America's Schools* (Kozol, 1992), *Their Highest Potential: An African-American School Community in the Segregated South* (Siddle-Walker, 1996), *Ghetto Schooling: A Political Economy of Urban Educational Reform* (Anyon, 1997), *Troubling the Angels: Women Living with HIV/AIDS* (Lather & Smithies, 1997), *Decolonizing Methodologies: Research and Indigenous Peoples* (Tuhiwai Smith, 1999), *A River Forever Flowing: Cross-Cultural Lives and Identities in the Multicultural Landscape* (He, 2003), *Red Pedagogy: Native American Social and Political Thought* (Grande, 2004), *Indigenous Storywork: Educating the Heart, Mind, Body, and Spirit* (Archibald, 2008), *Race Is—Race Isn't: Critical Race Theory and Qualitative Studies in Education* (Parker, Deyhle, & Villenas, 1999), and *Personal~Passionate~Participatory Inquiry into Social Justice in Education* (He & Phillion, 2008). The counternarratives are also demonstrated in Southern women writers' fiction such as *Their Eyes Were Watching God* (Hurston, 1937/1965/2000), *Strange Fruit* (Smith, 1944), *Killers of the Dream* (Smith, 1949/1961), *The Bluest Eye* (Morrison, 1970), and *The Color Purple* (Walker, 1982).

This dialogue on curriculum of the South originates from an exploration of the issue of place in *Curriculum as Social Psychoanalysis: The Significance of Place* (Kincheloe & Pinar, 1991), and continued in *An Indigenous Curriculum of Place* (Ng-A-Fook, 2007), *This Corner of Canaan: Curriculum Studies of Place & the Reconstruction of the South* (Whitlock, 2007), *The Autobiographical Demand of Place: Curriculum Inquiry in the American South* (Casemore, 2008), and other works outside the field of curriculum studies such as *Rooted in Place: Family and Belonging in a Southern Black Community* (Falk, 2004) and *Belonging: A Culture of Place* (hooks, 2009). This dialogue is further invigorated by the analyses of the South begun by William M. Reynolds and Julie Webber in *The Civic Gospel: A Political Cartography of Christianity* (2009), continues to emerge in *A Curriculum of Place: Understandings Emerging Through the Southern Mist* (Reynolds, 2013) and in narrative analyses of the life in the South in this book (Whitlock, 2013), *A Quiet Awakening: Spinning Yarns from Granny's Table in the New Rural South* (Haynes, 2013), *Are You Mixed? A War Bride's Granddaughter's Narrative of Lives In-Between Contested Race, Gender, Class and Power* (Janis, 2013), *Reaping What You Sow: Southern Culture, Black Traditions, and Black Women* (Mikell, 2013), and *Exile Curriculum: Compelled to Live In-Between* (He, 2013).

We applaud with our hearts and souls that Saundra Murray Nettles' innovative inquiries into the "necessary spaces"—"the richness of African American childhood in the South"—raise challenging questions, transcend inquiry boundaries, transgress orthodoxy and dogma, research silenced narratives of underrepresented or disenfranchised individuals and groups with hearts and minds, embody a particular stance in relation to power, freedom, and human possibility, and promote a more balanced and equitable human condition that embodies cultural, linguistic, and ecological diversity and plurality of identities of individuals, groups, tribes, and societies that is conducive to the flourishing of creative capacities that invigorate intellectual, emotional, moral, and spiritual existence for all.

References

Anyon, J. (1997). *Ghetto schooling: A political economy of urban educational reform.* New York, NY: Teachers College Press.

Anzuldua, G. (1987). *Borderlands: La frontera.* San Francisco, CA: Aunt Lute Foundation.

Anzaldua, G. (Ed.). (1990). *Making face, making soul: Creative and critical perspectives by women of color.* San Francisco, CA: Aunt Lute Foundation.

Archibald, J. (2008). *Indigenous storywork: Educating the heart, mind, body, and spirit.* Vancouver, Canada: University of British Columbia Press.

Ayers, W., Quinn, T., & Stovall, D. (Eds.). (2009). *Handbook of social justice in education.* New York, NY: Routledge.

Bateson, M. C. (1989). *Composing a life.* New York, NY: Atlantic Monthly Press.

Bell, D. (1992). *Faces at the bottom of the well: The permanence of racism.* New York, NY: Basic.

Casemore, B. (2008). *The autobiographical demand of place: Curriculum inquiry in the American South.* New York, NY: Peter Lang.

Cooper, A. J. (1988). *A voice from the south.* New York, NY: Oxford University Press.

Dewey, J. (1916). *Democracy and education.* New York, NY: Macmillan.

Dewey, J. (1933, April 23). Dewey outlines utopian schools. *New York Times,* p. 7. Also in Boydston, J. A. (Ed.). (1989). *The later works (1925–1953) of John Dewey* (Vol. 9, pp. 136–140). Carbondale: Southern Illinois University Press,.

Douglass, F. (1845/1968). *Narrative of the life of Frederick Douglass: An American slave.* New York, NY: Signet.

Falk, W. W. (2004). *Rooted in place: Family and belonging in a Southern Black community.* New Brunswick, NJ: Rutgers University Press.

Grande, S. (2004). *Red pedagogy: Native American social and political thought.* Lanham, MD: Rowman & Littlefield.

Gutiérrez, K. D., Rymes, B., & Larson, J. (1995). Script, counterscript, and underlife in the classroom: James Brown versus Brown v. Board of Education. *Harvard Educational Review, 65*(3), 445–471.

Haynes, A. (2013). *A quiet awakening: Spinning yarns from granny's table in the NEW rural South.* Charlotte, NC: Information Age.

He, M. F. (2003). *A river forever flowing: Cross-cultural lives and identities in the multicultural landscape.* Greenwich, CT: Information Age.

He, M. F. (2010). Exile pedagogy: Teaching in-between. In J. A. Sandlin, B. D. Schultz, & J. Burdick (Eds.), *Handbook of public pedagogy* (pp. 469–482). New York, NY: Routledge.

He, M. F. (2013). *Exile curriculum: Compelled to live in-between.* Charlotte, NC: Information Age.

He, M. F., & Phillion, J. (Eds.). (2008). *Personal~passionate~participatory inquiry into social justice in education.* Charlotte, NC: Information Age.

hooks, b. (2009). *Belonging: A culture of place.* New York, NY: Routledge.

Hurston, Z. N. (1937/1965/2000). *Their eyes were watching God.* New York, NY: HarperCollins.

Jacobs, H. (1861/2001). *Incidents in the life of a slave girl.* Mineola, NY: Dove.

Janis, S. E. (2013). *Are you mixed? A war bride's granddaughter's narrative of lives in-between contested race, gender, class, and power.* Charlotte, NC: Information Age.

Kincheloe, J. L., & Pinar, W. F. (Eds.). (1991). *Curriculum as social psychoanalysis: The significance of place.* Albany: Sate University of New York Press.

Kozol, J. (1992). *Savage inequalities: Children in America's schools.* New York, NY: Crown.

Lather, P., & Smithies, C. (1997). *Troubling the angels: Women living with HIV/AIDS.* Boulder, CO: Westview (Earlier edition self-published in Columbus, OH: Greyden Press, 1995).

Mies, M., & Shiva, S. (1993). *Ecofeminism.* Halifax, Nova Scotia, Canada: Fernwood.

Mikell, C. (2013). *Reaping what you sow: Southern culture, Black traditions, and Black women.* Charlotte, NC: Information Age.

Minh-Ha, T. T. (1989). *Woman, native, other: Writing postcoloniality and feminism* (Midland Books). Bloomington: Indiana University Press.

Mohanty, C. T. (2003/2005). *Feminism without borders: Decolonizing theory, practicing solidarity.* Durham, NC: Duke University Press.

Morrison, T. (1970). *The bluest eye.* New York, NY: Lume.

Narayan, U. (1997). *Dislocating cultures: Identities, traditions, and third world feminism.* New York, NY: Routledge.

Ng-A-Fook, N. (2007). *An indigenous curriculum of place.* New York, NY: Peter Lang.

Nussbaum, M. (1997). *Cultivating humanity: A classical defense of reform in liberal education.* Cambridge, MA: Harvard University Press.

Parker, L., Deyhle, D., & Villenas, S. (Eds.). (1999). *Race is—race isn't: Critical race theory and qualitative studies in education.* Boulder, CO: Westview.

Reynolds, W. (Ed.). (2013). *A curriculum of place: Understandings emerging through the Southern mist.* New York: Peter Lang.

Reynolds, W., & Webber, J. A. (2009). *The civic gospel: A political cartography of Christianity.* Rotterdam/Boston/Taipei: Sense.

Schubert, W. H. (2009). *Love, justice, and education: John Dewey and the Utopians.* Charlotte, NC: Information Age.

Schubert, W. H. (2010). Outside curriculum. In C. Kridel (Ed.), *Encyclopedia of curriculum studies* (pp. 624–628). Thousand Oaks, CA: Sage.

Shiva, V. (1993). *Monocultures of the mind: Perspectives on biodiversity and biotechnology.* Atlantic Highlands, NJ: Zed.

Siddle-Walker, E. V. (1996). *Their highest potential: An African-American school community in the segregated South.* Chapel Hill: University of North Carolina Press.

Smith, L. (1944). *Strange fruit.* San Diego, CA: Harvest.

Smith, L. (1949/1961). *Killers of the dream.* New York, NY: W. W. Norton.

Tuhiwai Smith, L. (1999/2005). *Decolonizing methodologies: Research and indigenous peoples.* New York, NY: Palgrave.

Ulich, R. (1955). Response to Ralph Harper's essay. In N. B. Henry. (Ed.), *Modern philosophies of education*, Fifty-fourth Yearbook (Part I) of the National Society for the Study of Education (pp. 254–257). Chicago, IL: University of Chicago Press.

Walker, A. (1982). *The color purple.* Orlando, FL: Harcourt.

Whitlock, R. U. (2007). *This corner of Canaan: Curriculum studies of place & the reconstruction of the South.* New York, NY: Peter Lang.

Whitlock, R. U. (2013). *Queer South rising: Voices of a contested place.* Charlotte, NC: Information Age.

Preface

Iwanted to be an architect as soon as I was old enough to understand the word. I watched my uncle, a student in architecture at Howard University, design and build models. I followed his example, first, with white plastic blocks from which I fashioned entire villages and later, a solar house for a science project in 1964. I had other, sometimes parallel childhood passions that I engaged in and imagined I could do as a career: reading, helping people learn, taking photographs and developing them, playing the piano, writing plays and newspaper articles.

I did not become an architect. My childhood excursions led me to different social roles and careers: librarian; wife and mother; scholar of African American Studies, human development, and education; research scientist; community activist. Since the 1960s, my foremost concern has been promoting the well-being of African American women and underserved children and youth, especially those in impoverished neighborhoods. Whenever I could, in my careers as well as in my family and community roles, I integrated my interest in place and space, seeking answers to such questions as, Which built, social, or natural aspects of place are important in the transmission of African American cultural heritage and values? What meanings do African American children and adults attach to different learning spaces? What roles did family members and neighbors play in creating nurturing physical and social spaces for children? How can community involvement be deployed to address pressing issues such as achievement and graduation gaps, environmental influences (such as toxic waste

Necessary Spaces, pages xvii–xxvii
Copyright © 2013 by Information Age Publishing
All rights of reproduction in any form reserved.

and violence) on school adjustment, and child health problems that affect cognitive and social development?

In pursuing answers to these questions, it now seems inevitable that I came upon architect Christopher Alexander's work. I had found references to his 1977 book, *A Pattern Language*, in many sources; the book resembles a hypertext with 253 design problems, each described in photographs, diagrams, empirical background, and instructions for solution. Here was a guide that I could use to "read" or interpret the built, natural, and social environments in terms of constituent components, from smaller elements, such as still water (swimming pools and ponds) and "your own home," to the more complex entities and concepts, such as agricultural valleys and the psychological life, as well as the requirements for community settings that support growth in each stage of life.

One entry, "Network of Learning," was especially compelling. Citing cultural critic Ivan Illich's (1971) proposal for "education without schools," Alexander and colleagues asserted that learning should be decentralized, and the network of learning defined by social and spatial dimensions. There would be "workshops, teachers at home or walking through the city, professionals willing to take the young on as helpers, older children teaching younger children, museums, youth groups traveling, scholarly seminars, industrial workshops, old people, and so on" (Alexander et al., 1977, p. 102). Alexander's visions for the network of learning brought to mind stories that friends, relatives, and I recall about our childhoods in segregated, economically diverse Black neighborhoods in the South, especially before the *Brown v. Board of Education* holding and in the decade or so afterwards. In our remembered networks, educational opportunities, including those in schools, were distributed across the continuum from informal to formal and from place to place. Moreover, the experiences we remember depicted not only our personal characteristics (such as our gender) but the mutual interplay between particular places or settings and people and their characteristics and messages.

As I write, I am reminded of shared memories at the funeral and repast for a beloved friend, Rosa Walker Murray (1916–2011), who lived in Baltimore most of her long life. Amid tears and smiles, the middle-aged children of Rosa's cohort talked about the Mother's Club that Rosa and other moms in the neighborhood had organized to learn about and try out the latest childrearing information. The mothers, their spouses, and other adults monitored children's activities from the front porches of their row houses. The tidy blocks of the neighborhood emanated pride of place, with roses and trimmed hedges in the small yards. Geraniums bloomed in large stone urns. Rosa conducted her own summer reading program, which required children to check out books from the Enoch Pratt Free Library, read the books, and give a detailed oral report. Rosa, a public school teacher and lifetime member of the NAACP and the Association for the Study of African American Life and History, especially encouraged reading on Black history.

*   *   *

In another way, I see my own research interests reflected in Alexander's vision. The conceptual framework that I use in my research and practice reflects my four decades of participating in and observing community life. The framework links community characteristics to academic achievement of children and youth in schools. I draw on descriptions of communities that function well (see, for example, Barbarin, 1981) and my work in the 1970s and 1980s with teams that evaluated the Cities in Schools program (Murray et al., 1980) and PUSH for Excellence programs (Murray Nettles, Murray, Gragg, Kumi, & Parham, 1982). The logic models of these programs were developed when a critical mass of scholars was theorizing about human ecology, the intricate interrelationships between individuals and the various environments (e.g., schools, families, and communities) in which children and adults live and grow. My conceptualization reflects the ecological perspectives of the times[1] and, like the programs we studied, can be applied to issues in Black education that practitioners and scholars consider to this day: the causes and solutions to Black-White disparities in achievement, disciplinary actions, and graduation rates; the unique historical circumstances of slavery and Jim Crow that influenced current conditions; and the need for social justice in education, including culturally relevant pedagogy.[2]

I define the community as an environment characterized by three features: structure, culture, and involvement. These features permit the use of "community" to refer to locales, such as neighborhoods, and to social interactions within and across locales. *Community structure* refers to the type and organization of the physical features and social units—such as educational resources and services, demographic characteristics, natural settings, the adequacy and arrangement of buildings and streets in the community, the layout and decoration of interior spaces, crowding, and other aspects of private and public places—within the community's boundaries. *Community culture*, or climate, encompasses the values, norms, and rules that serve to maintain community order and control, which facilitate extensive social interaction among community members and foster community members' personal and social development. I define *community involvement* as the actions (such as instruction, monitoring children's behavior, resource allocation, and mobilization) that individuals and organizations take to promote the development of children and youth, including investments of time and energy in experiences, which in turn influence behavioral and academic adjustment to school.

When I designed the framework, one of my motivations was to build conceptual bridges across disciplines and to provide information "that would be helpful in designing effective treatments and strengthening informal practices" (Nettles, 1991, p. 400). Since publishing the framework, I have worked with colleagues from different disciplines to understand the complexities of education in communities and schools. For example, while conducting a study of informal educators, I observed architect Janet Felsten's program, *Building on the Basics,* to foster participation in design among Baltimore children in an African American elementary school (Nettles, 1999). Sociologist James McPartland and I (McPartland & Nettles, 1991) carried out one of the first empirical studies of a mentoring program for seventh graders. Working with an interdisciplinary multi-university research team (developmental psychology, child and maternal health, and social epidemiology), I studied neighborhood effects on adjustment to school among first-grade African American and White children. We reported that *neighborhood community involvement with children* (*CIC*), a measure of connection defined as the degree of cohesion among community members and willingness of adults in the neighborhood to engage in collective socialization of children, was strongly associated with positive school adjustment (Caughy, Nettles, & O'Campo, 2007) and with fewer behavior problems in economically distressed neighborhoods (Caughy, Nettles, & O'Campo, 2008).

Necessary Spaces

In this interdisciplinary work and my readings of research and practice literature that describes conditions for optimal African American child development, I had noticed recurring experiences that emerged from children's everyday lives in communities. As I delved into other sources, including narratives of African Americans and writings on African American environmental thought, I noted many of the same qualities of experience. *Connection* is a broad category encompassing experiences of relatedness to others, to nature, to spiritual communities, and social institutions. *Practice* can occur through play and through rehearsal of skills. *Renewal* occurs in acts of reflection, play, and re-creation of mind, body, and spirit. *Exploration* includes experiences of discovery, independent travel, investigation, and taking a novel route. *Design* includes actions (such as problem definition, imagining, solution building, and getting feedback from others) conducted to shape the environment and the human experience.

Resistance refers to actions to understand, apply critical analysis, and oppose oppression, inequality, and inequity. Finally, *empowerment* includes experiences that increase the capacity of individuals to manage resources, make decisions, and develop a sense of personal control, mutual respect, and responsibility to others.

I use the metaphor "necessary spaces" to capture these experiences that consistently emerge from the interplay of physical, social, and psychological environments and the convergence of these qualities with contemporary notions of factors needed for optimal development of Black children. An example from the recent literature on connection comes from the American Psychological Association Task Force on Resilience and Strength in Black Children and Adolescents (2008). Resilience is a widely popular term for the individual's optimal functioning or positive adaptation leading to good outcomes in several areas of child development.[3] The Task Force identified communalism as one of the themes in its "portrait of resilience" for African American children and adolescents. According to the report of the Task Force, "Communalism includes the importance of social bonds and social duties, reflects a fundamental sense of interdependence and primacy of collective well-being, and offers the drive for connection and promotion within and across diverse groups" (p. 3). The Task Force report summarizes research on characteristics in the psychological space (such as the child's ability to regulate emotions, capacity for vicarious understanding or experience of another's feelings; and healthy sense of who one is as a Black person) that make for positive interactions with others.

Another example of a necessary space comes from the literature on empowerment. Tucker and Herman (2002) proposed self-empowerment theory (SET), which posits that academic success and behavior problems in African American children are influenced by self motivation to achieve, perceived self-control, and other factors consistent with self-regulation and autonomy. Two things are unique: the premise that African American students are especially in need of empowerment to offset the persistent social injustices they face, and the necessity of community mobilization, especially that which is based in the African American community. Community involvement provides the kinds of assistance and modeling recommended by the Partnership Education Program (PEP, the intervention based on self-empowerment theory), such as pairing positive feelings about the self with learning, management of negative emotions (as in conflict resolution training), and individualized academic tutoring.

The Committee on Community-Level Programs for Youth (National Research Council and Institute for Medicine, 2002) presented evidence for eight features of everyday settings that promote adolescent develop-

ment. Among them are features that pertain to connection ("Opportunities to Belong" and "Supportive Relationships"), empowerment ("Support for Efficacy and Mattering") and practice ("Opportunities for Skill
Building"). This Committee—composed of scholars, policymakers, and
practitioners—notes that the list of features is provisional in that it may
not include features that different cultural groups find important. Moreover, the features of settings are "really shorthand for saying that they are
features of the person's *interaction with* the setting.... It is the experience
of the adolescent-in-setting—the *processes* of interaction—that is critical to
development" (p. 88, emphasis in original).

Settings in which children participate in *design* are also characterized
by interaction, specifically between the physical context (including objects
and the surround itself), the social environment (people and problems
about the social context), and the child's personal characteristics. Sharon
Sutton, an African American architect and artist, conducts groundbreak-
ing research and practice in design education. Using data from observation, children's design activities, interviews, and archives, in *Weaving a Tapestry of Resistance: The Places, Power, and Poetry of a Sustainable Society*, Sutton
(1996) demonstrates that social/spatial conditions in neighborhoods and
elementary schools inform children's perspectives on the world. In other
work that uses the design charrette as a form of civic participation (Sutton
& Kemp, 2006), she finds that African American children produce imaginative proposals for transforming the social roles, spaces and places in neighborhoods.

Although research on the benefits of participation in design is in the
early stage, the available evidence is promising. For example, the Engineering Design Process is a component of the Engineering is Elementary
project to introduce engineering to students in grades 1–5. Using the
design process, historically underrepresented minorities in science, technology, engineering, and mathematics (STEM) fields were able to apply
the steps in the process to different contexts, such as conflict resolution,
in addition to STEM instructional activities. Teachers also described improvements in student work ethics and attitudes toward school (Moffett,
Weis, & Banilower, 2011).

Toward an Ecology of the Everyday Childhood Experiences in Southern Black Neighborhoods

My aim for this book was to capture the complexity and richness of education—the dynamics among the children, other people and their messages, and the places—in Southern, African American neighborhoods. I

also explore the ways in which neighborhood resources and remembered experiences influence behavioral and academic outcomes for children. I focus on the early school years, which are critical for success in schools. In *Early Warning! Why Reading by the End of the Third Grade Matters,* the Annie E. Casey Foundation (2010) summarizes evidence showing that the majority of children who read below grade level in third grade will continue to have problems in high school, not only with reading, but with social behavior and academic performance.

I focus on the South and concur with Jerome Morris and Carla Monroe (2009), who make the important observation that "most contemporary and educational studies ignore the South as a critical racial, cultural, political, and economic backdrop in Black education" (p. 21). Yet there are reasons why we should consider the educative process in schools and communities in the South. It is the cradle of the Black experience and foundational in the development of Black identities in North America and continues to be home for the majority of the Black population.

According to Jaynes and Williams (1989) nearly 90% of African Americans lived in the South at the beginning of the last century, although by 1970, this percentage had decreased to 53% due to migration of the population to the North and to other regions of the United States. In her book, *Call to Home: African Americans Reclaim the Rural South,* Carol Stack (1996) writes that, beginning in the 1970s, Blacks began to move from the North and West back to the South. While the Hispanic population has been increasing more in the South than in other parts of the United States, African American students remain the highest proportion of the growing numbers of students of color in the South. The Southern Education Foundation (2010) documents that in the public school population in Southern states,[4] the racial breakdown of the student population is 49% White, 27% African American, 20% Hispanic, 3% Asian/Pacific, and 1% Native American or other. Not only are students of color in the majority, but low-income children (eligible for free and or reduced-price lunch) make up half or more of children in public schools. Educational resources in the South are relatively poor as well. Data from the U.S. Census Bureau (2011) show that of the 14 Southern states, all except Delaware and Maryland are below the U.S. average per-pupil educational expenditures.

In my inquiry, I used these questions as guides: What are the social and physical contexts of neighborhood memories? What forms of remembered experiences emerge from the mutual influence of social, physical, and psychological environments? Throughout the inquiry I focused on three interdependent realms of children's everyday experiences described in Robin Moore and Donald Young's framework (1978) as "actually used and experienced by children": (a) physical, or physiographic space,[5] which includes objects, buildings, natural elements, and people; (b) social space of human relationships and culture, including family life, school settings, and peer relations; and (c) physiological-psychological space, the realm of body and mind, which includes gender, age, ethnicity, and other characteristics.

I decided to use my own environmental autobiography to structure the exploration, starting by recording my own and my family's memories of childhood experiences in three places in Georgia: Henry County, a once-rural area about 31 miles south of Atlanta; Paradise Park, a residential development in Clayton County that borders Fulton (of which Atlanta is the county seat); and Washington Park, an Atlanta neighborhood developed by Blacks for Blacks. These three places provide a unique opportunity for deep exploration of the formal and informal opportunities distributed within what Pierce Lewis (1979) and other geographers call the cultural landscape, or the landscape made, not by nature alone but through human activity. Rich archival sources exist for these places, particularly the Washington Park neighborhood, which was designated a historic district in 2000. Three of the individuals who participated in the network of learning there have published memoirs.

I broadened the inquiry through insights and findings from the literature of African American history, culture, and environmental thought, and other academic fields, such as psychology, sociology, architecture, and education, which have contributed to our understanding of physical and social environments for children and youth. I visited African American historical sites and read books and articles about landscapes, vernacular architecture, and material culture for general populations and for African Americans in particular. I examined published autobiographical writings, including those by W.E.B. Du Bois (1868–1963), Booker T. Washington (1856–1915), Mamie Garvin Fields (1888–1987), Zora Neale Hurston (1891?– 1960), Annie L. McPheeters (1907–1994), and Richard Wright (1908–1960). Living authors include educator Frances Pivott Robinson, journalist Charlayne Hunter-Gault, social activist Randall Robinson, and writers Ta-Nehisi Coates and Lorene Cary.[6]

The essays in this book interweave memories of necessary spaces with the development of the network of learning. The first essay, "Home Ground," describes my relationships with my parents, siblings, and grandparents in the Washington Park neighborhood, now a National Historic District. Another form of connection, the link to my immediate ancestral past, was fostered in the physical landscapes in and around McDonough, Georgia, the site of my ancestors' work as enslaved persons, peasants, and farmers. I reflect on lessons in design I learned in my childhood home and garden and discuss literature on learning in communities of enslaved people.

"Curriculum of Place" examines the rise of learning landscapes in the neighborhood and opportunities these places afforded for practice, renewal, exploration, and empowerment. In addition to my story, I weave experiences described in autobiographies of Black women and men. Homes, vacant lots, natural settings, schools, city blocks, places of business all served as places in which learners interacted with "community coaches," ordinary people who lived in neighborhoods and provided life lessons. In the autobiographies, I found awareness of constraints posed by race to be the most salient consideration, although women alluded to the constraints of gender roles.

"Landscapes of Resistance" considers the ways that children have contributed to the Black freedom struggle. I weave the roles of children, parents, community leaders, churches, and schools into narratives about the Civil Rights Movement, the War on Poverty, and a school whose principal resisted the negative labeling of the school and its students by creating a network inside the school.

"Necessary Spaces" is the culminating essay. I reflect on the themes in the previous essays and consider the ways in which environmental memories, both individual and collective, can be used in building neighborhood networks for lifelong learning in the 21st century.

*   *   *

I have lived in one state, Maryland, which had a large pro-Confederate minority, although the state remained part of the Union during the Civil War. I was born in Atlanta, Georgia, and returned to live in Savannah in my 50s. I am a Southern African American woman and a feminist; I am drawn to voices that respect strong community roles for girls and women. Like many Southern writers, I am moved to reflect upon and record my impressions of places and am curious about the ways that other people experience place and space.

Given my sensibilities and professional interests, the core of this inquiry is the central role of space in human welfare, particularly in teaching and learning. Although stories about the failings of parents, teachers, and community members are reported in journal articles, news reports, and proposals for funding, alternative narratives exist, ones that go beyond examples of socioeconomic conditions and abstract concepts to stories that seek to understand experiences of learners and teachers grounded in time and place. These narratives offer what I have learned about how neighborhood networks of lifelong learning have been influential in the past and how they can and must be restored to promote equality of educational opportunity and equity in educational outcomes for all.

Notes

1. Ecological theoretical perspectives emerged, particularly in the 1970s, from psychology and other disciplines. For example, in ecological psychology, Trickett and colleagues (Trickett & Moos, 1973; Trickett & Todd, 1972) examined social contexts of schools, including persons (teacher and student), locale (urban vs. rural), and school organization. In developmental psychology, Bronfenbrenner (1979) identified links (called mesosystems) between and among immediate contexts or microsystems (such as peers) of the developing person. One essential link is the family-school connection. In the research literature, the myriad phenomena constituting this relationship fall under various labels, among them parental involvement, home-school relations, family influences on school adjustment, school-community relations, community involvement, and family-school-community partnerships (see, for examples, Epstein, 2001; Sanders, 2006).

2. Through historical, theoretical, and qualitative inquiry, scholars are continuing to uncover important facts and insights in areas such as the achievement gap (Perry, Steele, & Hilliard, 2003), social justice in education (He & Phillion, 2008); culturally relevant pedagogy (Ladson-Billings, 2009), and predominantly Black schools in the post–Civil Rights era (Morris, 2004).

3. Research on resilience has deepened our understanding of how interrelated contexts can contribute to academic and psychosocial competence in children and youths. Resilience, typically defined as the individual's successful response to risk (Rutter, 1987), is increasingly described as a property of systems—school, home, community, healthcare—in reciprocal interaction with basic human adaptational systems, such as attachment, self-efficacy, and intelligence (Masten, 2001; Pianta & Walsh, 1998).

4. According to the U.S. Census Bureau, the South is made up of the following states: Alabama, Arkansas, Delaware, Florida, Georgia, Kentucky, Louisiana, Maryland, Mississippi, North Carolina, Oklahoma, South Carolina, Tennessee, Texas, Virginia, and West Virginia.

5. Although meanings of space vary, space-related concepts abound in scholarship from diverse disciplines. Economists, psychologists, and sociologists examine neighborhood effects on school achievement by statistically associating spaces, defined as census-based information of sociodemographic or structural features, with student performance on IQ and subject-matter tests. In education, curriculum theorists use space a metaphor for society (Schutz, 1997) and examine the significance of place as a way of knowing (Kincheloe & Pinar, 1991). Examples of place-conscious traditions abound in education, including pedagogy of place, outdoor education, experiential learning, and community-based education (Gruenewald, 2003; Hutchison, 2004). There is also a substantial literature on the design of formal learning spaces (Hutchison, 2004), as well as studies of place and literacy (see, for example, Kinloch, 2010; Neuman & Celano, 2001).

6. I used the narrative inquiry approach of Clandinin and Connelly (2000). Data sources included published autobiographical writings: *Up From Slavery: An Autobiography* (Washington, 1901); *Dusk of Dawn: An Essay Toward an Autobiography of a Race Concept* (Du Bois, 1940); *Dust Tracks on a Road: An Autobiography* (Hurston, 1942); *Black Boy (American Hunger): A Record of Childhood and Youth* (Wright, 2005); *Lemon Swamp and Other Places; A Carolina Memoir* (Fields, 1983); *Library Service in Black and White: Some Personal Recollections, 1921–1980* (McPheeters, 1988); *Black Ice* (Cary, 1991); *In My Place* (Hunter-Gault, 1992); *Defending the Spirit: A Black Life in America* (R. Robinson, 1999); *Is Urban Education too Hard for God?* (F. Robinson, 2000); and *The Beautiful Struggle: A Father, Two Sons, and an Unlikely Road to Manhood* (Coates, 2009). I augmented the autobiographies with oral histories, interviews, newspaper clippings, maps, photographs, histories of towns cited in the autobiographies, and descriptions of schools and other places. I selected the sources to reflect variation in time period, gender, locale (urban and rural), and occupation. I included my own environmental autobiography as well.

The initial analysis was based on procedures for qualitative data analysis described by Miles and Huberman (1994) and Chawla (1986). In the first stages of analysis, I isolated relevant texts from the autobiographies and supplemental documentation. I then assigned descriptive codes denoting specific physical environments (such as church and home), persons involved as teachers or learners, and activities undertaken and prepared a matrix for each individual (case). I re-read the original texts and each case entry in the matrix to code for type of remembered experience (for instance, sense of responsibility to others and feelings of efficacy) afforded by the learning environment (the physical space, the persons, and the activities). I sorted memories of experiences into seven broad categories (connection, design, practice, empowerment, exploration, resistance, and renewal), which represented recurring patterns I noted in the research and practice literature. I developed time-ordered matrices and prepared the first draft, a narrative of the development of the network of learning over time. I integrated insights and findings from the place conscious and ecological perspectives, noted above, as well as the case descriptions. The findings are reported as a narrative of the development, decline, and restoration of the network, integrated with findings regarding the qualities of experience and the content and structure of the learning environment.

Acknowledgements

O ver the years, I have explored communities as environments for psychosocial and intellectual development of children and youths. The essays in this book are based on the social and physical legacies of African Americans in the South that I have presented at conferences, in various writings, and in public lectures. I am indebted to anonymous reviewers of my papers on aspects of African American networks of learning presented at the annual conferences of the American Educational Research Association; the American Psychological Association Society for Environmental, Population, and Conservation Psychology; and the Environmental Design Research Association. I especially appreciate the invitation from Brian Katen and the Department of Landscape Architecture to present my work in progress at Virginia Tech's Women and Minority Artists and Scholars Lecture Series. The audience feedback was invaluable. Portions of Chapter 3 are excerpts from my chapter, "Examining School-Community Connections Through Stories," in *Narrative and Experience in Multicultural Education*, edited by JoAnn Phillion, Ming Fang He, and F. Michael Connelly (reprinted by permission of SAGE Publications).

This project extended over many years, and I thank friends, colleagues, and family who have supported and assisted me. Special thanks go to my husband, Ronald W. Bailey, and daughters, Alana and Kali Murray, who read many drafts of the essays and offered critical and insightful comments and suggestions. Over breakfasts, lunches, and tea, Betty Franklin helped me identify aspects of the writing that were unclear or cliché d, but she always pointed out the parts she liked and ways to strengthen the work. Fran Young, Janet Felsten, and Barbara Wasik are constant sources of inspiration for inquiry on the importance of place and space in children's everyday lives.

Dr. Martha T. Mednick, an emerita professor of psychology at Howard University and my doctoral mentor, introduced me to research on academic achievement among African Americans and to advocacy for social justice. She has supported me throughout my career as a scholar, and I am deeply grateful to her.

1

Home Ground

Consider Henry Ossawa Tanner's *The Banjo Lesson*. The painting depicts a sparsely furnished room, its walls and plank floors bathed in golden light. Here are a wooden table and chair in the background, a rug, a hat, and cooking utensils on the floor. You know quickly it is the interior of a house, a simple cabin—home ground. There, a dark, bearded man, middle-aged, maybe older, sits on a stool, legs spread wide. A boy, perhaps 8 or 9 leans against one of the man's legs and strums a banjo with this right hand. The boy and the man both look intently at the face of the African banjo, their cheeks almost touching. Art historians Romare Bearden and Harry Henderson (1993) interpret this painting as a depiction of the transmission of African American culture. The observer sees the relationships to each generation and to this artifact of heritage, an instrument basic to the rhythms of community life.

For me, connection in this and other ways unfolded on my home ground, Atlanta's Washington Park neighborhood. As Grey Gundaker (1998) writes in the introduction to *Keep Your Head to the Sky: Interpreting African American Home Ground*, "the crucial investment that makes a place

Necessary Spaces, pages 1–20

1

home ground is not investment of money but of connections, of roots; thus land becomes the place of happenings: births, deaths, labor, friendships, disputes, and goings and comings of the generations" (p. 15). On home ground, I had my first experiences as a learner, with family and neighbors as my educators. There, among myriad imaginative encounters, I discovered my immediate ancestral roots and how they were strengthened as networks of learning originated and spread in Black American communities.

Washington Park

My immediate family, which included my parents, my sister, and my brother, lived with my father's parents (George E. Rice and Beulah Weems Rice) on Desoto Street in Atlanta. Our house in Atlanta started out as a bungalow in the neighborhood known (in tribute to the educator Booker T. Washington) as Washington Park (Figure 1.1). Located about 2 miles west of Atlanta's central business area, the neighborhood had been developed early in the 1920s, largely by two enterprising Black men, Herman Perry and Daniel Chennault (Washington Park—A History, 1999). Whites were reluctant to move to the west side (although the first of four separate subdivision plans for White residents had been proposed as early as 1906, and an elementary school, the Ashby Street School, had been constructed in 1910 for White children). The plans for White settlement came to a halt in 1919 when the Parks Department of Atlanta designated several acres as the first recreational area for African Americans in the city. The 25-acre park, named Washington Park, was completed in 1928 and had several pavilions, a swimming pool, and playing fields (Georgia Department of Natural Resources, 2000). The houses in the Washington Park neighborhood departed from the shotgun styles typical of Black neighborhoods of the time and included elegant Tudors, bungalows like ours, and brick two-story forms that seemed to convey a no-nonsense attitude.

In 1917, when my grandparents married, they joined the great surge of African Americans who moved northward from the rural South. The Rice family did not go far from their home grounds in rural Henry County and Clayton County, Georgia; they went to Atlanta. I interviewed my father (George H. Rice) in 1989, and he identified five different houses in which the family had lived, beginning with the house, on Raymond Street, in which he was born in 1923. The second move in 1924 was to a house across the street from Booker T. Washington.

The high school, built in 1924, was the first high school for Blacks in Atlanta. The school, the alma mater of Martin Luther King Jr., is within the area immediately adjacent to the official boundaries of Washington Park and is a

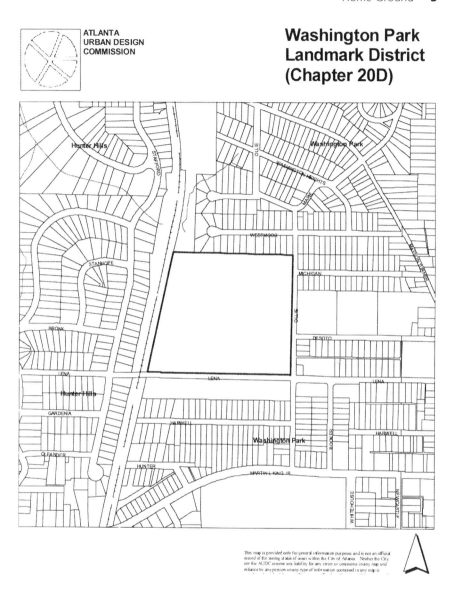

ATLANTA
URBAN DESIGN
COMMISSION

Washington Park
Landmark District
(Chapter 20D)

Figure 1.1   Washington Park Landmark District. *Source:* www.atlantaga.gov

massive brick structure; with its playing fields, it occupies a very large city block. One-story brick and frame houses stand neatly across the street, originally called C Street. Graham Jackson (the accordionist who serenaded President Franklin D. Roosevelt at Warm Springs, Georgia) had the name changed to White House Drive. Jackson's own house was a replica of the Little White House at

Figure 1.2   Ronald W. Bailey. Booker T. Washington Statue at Washington High School, Atlanta, Georgia, 2006.

Warm Springs, hence the name change. From the lawn of Jackson's house, you could see the statue of Booker T. Washington "lifting the veil" that represented ignorance (Figure 1.2). The statue is a replica of the monument at Tuskegee University (formerly Tuskegee Institute); Washington was its first principal.

My grandfather sold his house (to Jackson) and moved the family to two different rentals.

The Great Depression took the Rice family down until 1933, when my grandfather moved for the last time to a bungalow he bought on Desoto Street. There, the family actively altered the bungalow to incorporate a multigenerational space. My grandfather and his two sons had dug a basement by the time I was born in 1947. The basement had a living room, bedroom, bath, kitchen, a

Figure 1.3   Ronald W. Bailey. Rice Family Home in Washington Park Historic District, 2006.

darkroom for my father, and a tiny studio that housed my uncle's drafting table and the models of houses he created from balsa wood. I lived with my mother and father in the basement apartment until I was 3 or 4, when the men in my family built a nine-room apartment over the first floor where my grandparents lived, and we moved upstairs. My uncle and his family moved to the basement. One year, the screened front porch was enclosed to expand the living room on my grandparent's floor. Thus, our house (Figure 1.3) in Washington Park had three generations under one roof, and the designers (my grandfather and his sons) made spaces for connection between family members.

The living room/dining room combination on my grandparent's floor deepened multigenerational space. Here, Sunday dinners were spread for the people who lived in the house and in other houses. Interior and exterior stairways led to the two upper floors and the basement. Little ones could visit freely, but doors could be closed off for privacy and safety when desired or necessary. In the summer, children in the neighborhood liked to play in our basement (it was cool there) and in our backyard, which I recall as a more interesting space than others in the neighborhood. A lean-to was attached to the garage. This was our playhouse for school and other activities; the garage was off limits to children and apparently, to cars as well—it housed power saws, other tools, sheet rock, and lumber. A swing set stood outside and next to it, a large, prolific fig tree. Behind the garage were spaces for animals (we always kept dogs in the yard) and a vegetable garden. We used the rest of the backyard for a clothesline and flowers.

I think the yard resembled the home grounds that landscape architect Richard Westmacott (1992) describes in his book on African American yards and gardens in the rural South. Our yard had definite functions, with areas for subsistence (growing vegetables, raising chickens and ducks), leisure and recreation, and ornament and display. One Easter weekend (I was 7 or 8), my grandfather brought some unclaimed boxes from the post office that contained baby chicks and ducklings. We children identified a handful of the chickens as pets (the rest of the animals were housed behind the garage) and cared for them in the house until they lost their fuzz.

When the animals became mature birds, they outgrew the backyard spaces. I thought we would give them away, perhaps to a farmer. My grandmother had other ideas; she summoned her rural ways, chopped off their heads, and threw the bodies into a metal trash can until the noise of their flapping subsided. The birds were frozen for meals. Time passed until I was able to eat chicken prepared in our house; I rarely eat duck.

I learned how plants grow, how chickens and ducks are killed, how puppies can thrive and sometimes die, and that fruit can grow on vines.

* * *

In the house that Black men constructed and remodeled, I would carry a box of white interlocking plastic bricks to different rooms, downstairs and up, building simple houses and towers. I tried to draw houses, but my drawings were flat.

"How do I make my houses look like real ones?" I asked my uncle one day. He was home for a break from Howard University, where he studied architecture.

His exact response is somewhere buried deep in my brain. Knowing his propensity for demonstration, perhaps he took my hand, guiding it in a slant from a point in the corner of the page to the center, turned my hand downward to draw one line and then another, until a box emerged, voluminous in its dimensions, hinting at hidden spaces just beyond my eye's view.

Or, he would have recited, "Drip, drip, drip/you are a San Drip," the little poem he always muttered affectionately as a preface, and then, "You gotta know how to use perspective."

Knowing how I loved big words, he probably had spelled it out. "You pick your point, and then draw lines to make it seem like your house has sides and a front." I practiced daily until I could put my little compositions in perspective. As I struggled to master that technique, I decided I wanted to be an architect.

Talking with my uncle Ronald, watching, and imitating him were occasions for my informal apprenticeship in design. There were others to come as well. I didn't know it at the time, but my dad had bought land in a place called Paradise Park; it was close to Henry County and the ancestral home ground. He was drawing plans for a single-family house.

My father, who had learned photography from his uncle Ellie Weems, had several old cameras and a darkroom in the basement. He taught me to snap people and places with a Brownie and stand by him in the dark before trays of chemicals, making images from rolls of celluloid. High school students, in the Camera Club that my father advised, would come over to our house sometimes to use the darkroom (the school had none). Now, I see him as a young man, say or 27 or 28; he was short, with brown skin and thick hair made unmovable with pomade. My brother George and I resemble him. I think my sister looks like my mother, who was an inch or two shorter than my father. My favorite image is the family portrait (Figure 1.4) that my uncle, Ellie Weems, photographed in his Jacksonville studio.

Following her mother, my mother was an expert seamstress and made most of our clothes (including the ones in the portrait). My parents made a beautiful, life-size rag doll for me when I was about a year old. But the doll, which I remember vividly, was one of the first manufactured Black baby dolls. She had "AMOSANDRA" embossed on her back; she could drink from a miniature bottle and soon after, wet her diaper. I thought she was named after me. When I was an adult, I learned that the doll depicted the baby in the Amos 'n' Andy show, a radio program (with Whites in the title roles) and then a controversial television show. Sometimes, my parents allowed us to watch, but in our house, the stereotypical images and language were off limits.

One Christmas, Santa Claus brought my sister and me a real sewing machine, scaled down to a child's hands. My mother helped us to cut patterns for doll clothes and guided our fingers as we tried to make seams. Indeed, our house on Desoto Street sometimes resembled a giant workroom, with painting and other improvements to the physical structure, sewing and tailoring (my uncle and father were handy with the needle, making vinyl slipcovers), and woodworking going on most of the time. My grandfather, "Papa," as we called him, liked to make cornice boards.

Some of this activity was for the love of design, including aesthetics with recycling resources, bettering our circumstances, saving money for the things that family wages and bartering could not acquire. Every adult

Figure 1.4   Ellie L. Weems. George H. Rice, Sr. Family, 1956. *Source:* Personal collection of Saundra Rice Murray Nettles.

worked outside the home: Papa as a postal clerk, mama and daddy as teachers. While my parents were away, grandmamma took care of my younger brother and kept an eye on my sister and me after we came home from school. Sometimes, and I don't know how she fit this in (taking my brother with her perhaps?), she worked as a domestic for White families who gave her hand-me-down clothing for us. (We preferred the ones we made at home). When she was at home, she hooked rugs, planned and planted flowerbeds and vegetable gardens, cooked and canned, and raised chickens, rabbits, and ducks. I would stand right next to her, helping in any way she would allow—digging a little hole, patting soil around seedlings, measuring sugar and sifting flour for cakes, cutting squares for the quilts she made from old dresses and skirts. Home was a buzzing haven, with everyone pitching in to make it beautiful and welcoming.

When she writes in *Yearning*, bell hooks (1990) could have been describing my grandmother, and to a different extent, my mother, who taught Black children in schools:

> Then they returned to their homes to make life happen there. This tension between service outside one's home, family, and kin network, service provided to white folks which took time and energy, and the effort of black women to conserve enough of themselves to provide service (care and nurturance) within their own families and communities is one of the many factors that has historically distinguished the lot of black women in patriarchal white supremacist society from that of black men. (p. 42)

Yet, as I child, I glimpsed the racial aspect of that tension between work and service among the men of my family. Although Papa had a middle-class job (as a postal worker) by the Black community's standards, I heard White coworkers, when I visited his workplace, speak of George as a "good boy." On Saturdays, when my father drove us around town on errands, I witnessed the ways that Whites treated him—putting change on the counter instead of the palm of his open hand, for example.

Most of the time, I did not have face-to-face encounters with White people, even when I was on White property, when my family visited my grandfather's brother, Uncle Willie, and his wife, Aunt Clara. They lived in a small house on the grounds of an estate in northeast Atlanta. He was the chauffeur and she the cook/housekeeper for a wealthy White couple. I knew that this neighborhood was different from ours; I had never seen streets so wide and smoothly paved nor any houses so large or with so many trees and flowers. Our street was unpaved, perhaps into the 1950s. Our family was not permitted to go near the mansion; we confined our visits to the interior of the small house on the back of the property. Aunt Clara would treat us to delicious food served on china, iced tea and water in crystal; we ate with silver spoons and forks.

At home, on weekend mornings, I would tiptoe downstairs and have breakfast with my grandparents. I would sit at their white metal table in the kitchen and reach for hot biscuits and jelly, and grandma had made just for me something she called "keltea," a mixture of milk, sugar, and a spoonful of coffee. I drank it from a regular cup and saucer, feeling very grown-up.

Clare Cooper Marcus (1995), in the book *House as a Mirror of Self: Exploring the Deeper Meaning of Home*, writes about this kind of setting as a place for nurturance, one that "may have little to do with architecture or location but it has a lot to do with human love, warmth, and caring" (p. 45). Before children develop an expansive awareness of and deep attachment to place, their great need is to dwell in the immediate environment of supportive adults in their families. For me, keltea with my grandparents represented the nurturing aspect of connection, but drinking keltea was also the occasion for imagining that I was drinking real coffee instead of sugar milk and that manipulating the physical objects (the cup and saucer) had magically turned me into an adult-like creature. In his essay, "Space, Place, and the Child," Yi-Fu Tuan (1977) tells us, "The child's imagination is of a special kind. It is tied to activity" (p. 33). Sharing nurturing space and preparing for adulthood was, of course, my activity in the moment.

Looking back, I have surmised that keltea was a concoction that my grandmother imported from her home ground: it was a symbol of rural, perhaps African American culture. The intergenerational ritual of keltea time established a bond that made other interactions possible, such as the one that centered on the two photographs and the story my grandmother told about the people depicted in the images of Figure 1.5—freed persons Alex and Carrie Weems.

Rural Georgia

In 1895, amid racial unrest in the South, Booker T. Washington (1895) gave a speech (now called the "Atlanta Compromise") at the Cotton Statesand International Exposition in Atlanta. Washington exhorted African

Figure 1.5 Ellie L. Weems. Alex and Carrie Weems, ca. 1920s. *Source:* Personal collection of Saundra Rice Murray Nettles.

Americans to "Cast down your bucket where you are.... Cast it down in agriculture, mechanics, in commerce, in domestic service, and in the professions" (p. 1), and to Whites, "Cast down your bucket among these people who have, without strikes and labor wars, tilled your fields, cleared your forests, builded your railroads and cities, and brought forth treasures from the bowels of the earth" (p. 1).

At the time of the Exposition, my great-great-grandparents, Alex and Carrie Weems, were freed persons, farming land in McDonough, Georgia. Alex died in 1940, in his 80s; Carrie lived until 1953, when I was 6 years old. The two of us were friends in the way that the very old and very young can be. She was bent with osteoporosis—we saw eye to eye. But the image of Carrie that I know is fixed. She stands alone in a cotton field, a middle-aged woman wearing a knit skullcap and holding a large round basket of cotton bolls. She is staring intently into the distance. The image, displayed prominently on the wall of my grandmother's den with a companion photograph of Alex—head bent, his white beard and sideburns framing his gentle, black features—was part of my childhood surround linking me to the cultural and economic past.

Carrie and Alex were my first encounters with enslaved people; my grandmother, Beulah Weems Rice, told me that they were her grandparents and that he was of mixed race. I have sought clues to the mysteries of their lives ever since: as a scholar, teaching and investigating the history of African American education; as a librarian, in the stacks of the Library of Congress and the Moorland-Spingarn Collection, where I read slave narratives and held crumbling photographs carefully in my hands; in Georgia and U.S. archival records. I found clues in one of those records—the *Slaveowners Census, Henry County, Georgia 1850* (Moore, 1964)—which listed T. D. Weems as the owner of 25 slaves and three other Weems men as owners of between 11 and 17 slaves.

Reading this, I had surmised that one of them had owned my ancestors. The Weems had one of the largest plantations in Henry County; their lands were located near the post office called Bear Creek Station, later renamed Hampton. In the 1870 census of the Bear Creek District in Henry County (Turner, 1995), Alex is listed as Ellick, 19 years of age, a male farmhand of mixed ancestry. He lived with Dorcas, his 37-year-old mother (a housekeeper and also of mixed ancestry) and Moses Weems, a Black man from Virginia. The dwelling number for the Moses Weems family was 857; Thomas D. Weems, a slave owner and his wife were listed in dwelling number 856.[1]

Early Networks of Learning

At 16 years of age, Alex was listed in the 1870 Census as unable to read or write, but by 1880, the census taker recorded that Alex was literate and that he lived with Carry (Carrie). She was 23, but could neither read nor write. Subsequent census records show that she remained illiterate. Until the end of the 18th century, only a small proportion of the total population in America had gone to schools. People became literate through such means as private tutoring and, particularly in New England, through religious instruction. According to the Schomberg Center for Research in Black Culture (2000), as early as 1638, for example, the Collegiate School was established in the Dutch colony of New Amsterdam (later New York City) to train Dutch and Black youth "in the knowledge of Jesus Christ." Nearly seven decades later in New York, Elias Neau opened in his home a school for religious instruction of Black children and adults. Beginning in the late 1700s, in antebellum Savannah, Georgia, a small number of free Blacks ran their own schools, and Black churches (among them the First African Baptist Church, constituted in 1777) conducted religious instruction for children (Johnson, 1995). In Charleston, South Carolina, free people of color operated schools (Johnson & Roark, 1984). As Wilma King (2005) writes in *African American Childhoods: Historical Perspectives From Slavery to Civil Rights*, "How free boys and girls gained literacy varied widely across regions and classes. In the absence of suitable public schools, persons with the financial wherewithal hired private tutors, sent their children away to school, or relocated entire families" (p. 63). Other free children of color taught themselves to read, write, or calculate; family members also offered instruction.

John Rury (2004) says in *Education and Social Change*, "Education was largely an informal affair, embedded in a host of other social relationships and guided by the necessities of life and work in the New World" (p. 43). Children and youth learned the skills needed for everyday life—hunting, farming, preparing and preserving food, sewing, cooking, making baskets and tools, building—in the family, through formal apprenticeship and in churches. For example, among African-born enslaved people in colonial America, the native born and overseers taught newcomers to speak the language of the master (Blassingame, 1979). In the informal sphere, the African-born enslaved served as teachers. For example, Blacks guided the technology of rice cultivation in the early years. As early as 1690, African slaves introduced baskets, known as fanners, to winnow hulled rice, as well as other aspects of rice cultivation, such as the method of planting seed. African Americans also taught the planters irrigation methods and brought seeds, which became staples such as okra and peas. Early methods of making baskets survive in the low country around Charleston (Gomez, 1998; Pollitzer, 1999).

Schools for Whites and free people of color became more widely available in the 19th century, but informal learning continued in communities of the enslaved. In *Deep Like the Rivers*, Thomas L. Webber (1978) examined slave testimonials from 1831 to 1865. From these narratives, he constructed a picture of slave education, which he defined as "the knowledge, attitudes, values, skills and sensibilities which an individual, or a group, consciously or unconsciously, has internalized" (p. xi). Webber identified nine themes that characterized the lessons that adult members transmitted to the young: communality, aversion to Whites, the distinction between true Christianity and slaveholding piety, the moral and behavioral superiority of Blacks, the power of Whites, the importance of family, belief in the spirit world, the desire for literacy, and the immense value of freedom.

When Webber read the narratives for the sources of education, he uncovered a network of learning in the slave quarters. The physical setting was the slave quarters, a set of houses and gardens set off from the main house of the plantation owners, although work houses—tannery, smithy, barns—were also sites of enslaved labor. In the quarters and other places on the plantations, families, children's peers, the slave community, and slave owners educated slaves, passing along skills, such as ironwork and quilting, and attitudes, such as the desire to be literate, the distinction between true Christianity and slaveholding piety, and the value of freedom. James D. Anderson (1988) tells us that, between 1800 and 1835, even slaveholders were forbidden from teaching slaves. During this period, most of the Southern states had passed laws making it a crime to teach slaves to read and write. Perhaps out of sight of the masters, an estimated 5% of slaves had become literate when the Civil War began (Anderson, 1988; Berlin, Favreau, & Miller, 1998).

According to the prevailing narrative of the time, benevolent Whites and the Freedman's Bureau were the primary impetus for the founding and spread of schools for ex-slaves, who in bondage were rarely afforded an education. Anderson (1988) and Heather Andrea Williams (2005) tell a different story, citing evidence that freedmen were in the forefront of a movement to establish universal schooling in the postwar South. Anderson writes that the freedmen's educational involvement was "rooted deeply within their own communal values" (p. 9) and reflected their intense desire to learn. Anderson called this movement the first crusade for common schools. Williams (2005) uses narratives, other primary sources, and publications to tell the story of how African Americans were agents in altering the landscape of education in the South. As slavery ended, literate freed people played leading roles as teachers and organizers of political conventions and schools. The difficulties of acquiring or constructing buildings suitable for use as schools led to the establishment of schools in other spaces, such as churches and private homes.

One example of agency comes from rural southeast Georgia (Brooks, n.d.). In Bullock County, three families of freed persons founded the Willow Hill School in 1874. The families owned the land, acquired through a work-trade agreement; they cleared the land, donated the land for the school, and converted a turpentine shanty into a one-room schoolhouse. Georgiana Riggs, a daughter in one of the families, was the first teacher. She was 15 years old and taught basic literacy and Bible reading. A board of trustees was eventually established to oversee the financial aspects of the school.

The school was moved to better and larger sites, first in 1890 and again in 1895. The community raised funds to build a school under the Rosenwald School-building program, which was implemented at Tuskegee Institute from 1914–1920 (Hoffschwelle, 2006). (Records show that the total cost of the two-teacher Willow Hill school building was $1,507, of which African American citizens raised $1,107; the Rosenwald Fund contributed $250; and the public schools contributed $150.)[2]

In rural Henry County where the Weems lived, churches were perhaps the primary sites for in-school teaching and learning. A Henry County historian writes, "A Mr. Wilson set up the first school for colored children in Henry County in 1866" (Rainer, 1971, p. 372), but the site is not named. Construction of the first public school for Black children (the McDonough Public School) did not begin until 1899; the school opened the next year with seven grades. In 1920, the high school department was added. The evidence is sparse, but at least 2 of Alex and Carrie's 14 children were educated. Her obituary states that their eighth child, Julia Weems Demery, "received her early education in McDonough, Georgia and attended Fort Valley Teachers Training School." Her youngest brother, Troy Weems, had enough education to qualify for and serve in the U.S. Army during World War I.

Like many freedmen, Alex was a peasant (the 1880 Census simply lists him as "at home" and married), most likely either a sharecropper or a tenant farmer. In *Homecoming: The Story of African American Farmers*, Charlene Gilbert and Quinn Eli (2000) tell us that by 1890, some 90% of Black farmers were sharecroppers. (These authors explain the difference between sharecropping and tenancy. Sharecroppers received a portion of the harvested crops in return for labor, whereas tenant farmers annually paid cash to the landowner and kept the remainder from the crops their labor produced.) My father's oral history interview notes that Alex obtained land of his own. Later, he gave a parcel to his eldest son, my great-grandfather Ellie, who had married Sallie Sutton, daughter of a former slave from Washington-Wilkes County in Georgia. The couple owned 30 acres of land in McDonough, on which they grew corn, wheat, sugar cane, watermelons, and peach trees for basic needs, and cotton for profit. Ellie built their house. Ellie and Sallie's children—Ellie Lee Jr. and Beulah, my grandmother—attended public schools in McDonough. After graduating, Ellie Lee Jr. studied photography at Tuskegee; my grandmother attended Fort Valley High and Industrial School in Fort Valley, Georgia. Tuskegee followed the model of the Hampton Normal and Agricultural Institute (founded in 1868). Booker T. Washington, who attended Hampton, strongly advocated this model, which featured academic instruction at a basic level, in service to technical and trade training (e.g., brickmaking, shoemaking) believed to maintain the subordinate status of Blacks in the Southern economy.

John W. Davison, a graduate of Atlanta University, founded my grandmother's school (Fort Valley High and Industrial School, now Fort Valley State University) in 1890. According to Anderson (1988), "The institution was chartered specifically to promote the 'higher and mental and manual training' of black students, but principal Davison was concentrating mainly on the development of a good liberal arts secondary and normal school for the training of black teachers" (p. 117). By contrast with Tuskegee, Atlanta University had such a program for teacher education. However, by 1917, when my grandmother had graduated, Fort Valley's survival as an institution required it to adopt the industrial model. Anderson writes, "Every student had to major in some form of menial labor such as laundering, cooking, or the care and cultivation of fruit trees" (p. 130). I surmise that my grandmother majored in the domestic arts.

At 20 years of age, she married my grandfather, George Rice (a teacher in Ellenwood, Georgia, and son of farmers); she had already returned to McDonough and taught briefly. When they married, she moved with Papa to Atlanta, where a year later the first of their five children was born. Papa, a graduate of Atlanta Baptist College (later, Morehouse College), began a long career as a clerk in the U.S. Postal Service, but grandmamma did not return to teaching. Occasionally, she worked as a domestic, earning a substantial portion of the funds to pay tuition for her children to attend historically Black liberal arts colleges (Spelman, Morris Brown, Morehouse, Clark, and Howard). Tuitions in those days were very low.

These days, I wonder how my grandmother's life might have unfolded had Fort Valley kept its liberal arts orientation, or had she foregone the industrial training that constrained her aspirations. But lives in her times, more so than in mine, were shaped by opportunity, race, gender, class, and place. Her brother, Ellie Lee Weems, studied photography at Tuskegee under Cornelius M. Battey,[3] the photographer whose subjects included Frederick Douglass, Booker T. Washington, and W. E. B. Du Bois. Uncle Ellie became a respected photographer in Jacksonville, Florida, where he operated a studio from 1929 until 1980, when he came to live with my father. With the industrial model, Ellie Weems attained a skill that contributed to his mobility. He loved his work and took advanced courses whenever he could. My father earned money for college as Ellie's apprentice (and introduced himself to my mother when she came to the studio for a portrait).

Connection

As a child, I would visit the home places (including Jacksonville, where the Lewis family, my mother's parents and siblings, settled after moving from Charleston) that were special to my grandparents and other kin. Sometimes these were occasions for nature lessons: how to pull cotton from the bolls and learning that it was a plant before it was a piece of cloth; how to keep biting into a muscadine grape until its skin burst and the sweetness rushed up your tongue, and learning that grapes grew on vines before people bought them in the grocery store; learning that water could come not only from spigots, but from wells dug deep in the ground. I participated (in a childlike way) in the rituals—the burials of relatives, the gathering of plants and fruits, drawing water from a well. When my mother's father passed, his body was laid out in the living room. I visited the room every chance I could get, moving close to the casket and listening for a ticking sound. The adults had told me that he died from a "clock in his leg"; after I told them I had not heard a thing, my mother explained that he had had a blood clot. Even though, at 4 years old, I did not know what that meant, the explanation made sense because I knew that events associated with blood could be very painful.

These were small, but profound lessons, of the kind that poet and memoirist Thylias Moss (1998) learned from her father. One day, watching him take a bird nest from a gutter, she recalled, "The universe became comprehensible the moment he touched it. For those few minutes, all meaning relocated inside two eggs that already held rock dove embryos, yet there was no crowding. Meaning fit perfectly, the nucleus it should be" (p. 24).

* * *

Now, more than a half-century later, when I visit Henry County to gather data for a genealogy or to visit ancestral gravesites, I encounter home ground in my imagination, replacing the suburban sprawl I literally see from I-75 with abiding memories of hills, small farms, and roads that curve gently. On one of those research trips in 2006, I decided to look for the plantation that the Weems slaves had farmed. It is a local landmark, and the person at the tourist information center knew exactly where to direct me. Before my visit, I had discovered in a history of Henry County a black and white photograph that showed a gracious plantation house (Rainer, 1971). The caption explained that the house was built in 1848 by Thomas Dickson Weems in the Southern Colonial style, and in 1923 a porch and a 4-column portico had been added. An ad that appeared when the house was up for sale in 2012 says the property had an intact "organic kitchen garden and the smoke house, and the carriage house. The plantation house is described as "a beautiful romantic house with large foyer and spacious rooms" (Property Nut, 2011).

When I drove to the site and glimpsed the remaining outbuildings, I was reminded of how the landscape of slave quarters might have highlighted the importance of the family and communality—two themes that emerged in *Deep Like the Rivers*, Thomas Webber's 1978 analysis of education among slaves. On many plantations, the cabins tended to be a distance from the main house, assuring, for instance, that children could see parents in roles beyond their work as slaves. James Blassingame (1979) wrote of the enslaved child and father: "In the quarters, for example, where he saw his parents most often, his father acted like a man, castigating whites for their mistreatment of him, being a leader, protector, and provider" (p. 190). Also, on many plantations, slave houses in the quarter were close together in a row or semicircle. Children could play games within the watchful gaze of other peers or of the slave assigned to nursery duties. Depending on the plantation, the quarters could be the site of religious instruction, control of behavior, group solidarity, and recreation. "Recreational activities," writes Blassingame, "led to 'cooperation, social cohesion, tighter communal bonds,' and brought all classes of slaves together in common pursuits" (p. 106).

The map of my home ground of Washington Park contained vestiges of the rural spaces of my father's ancestors (the Weems and the Rice families) and included the towns of Hampton, Locust Grove, and McDonough in Henry County, and Ellenwood and Morrow in Clayton County, Georgia. All lie within the original boundaries of Henry County, about 20 miles south of Atlanta. My grandparents had brought their own particular customs and objects when they migrated to Atlanta. The fabric in my home ground of Washington Park also made for close ties. According to descriptions in the announcement of listing in the National Register of Historic Places

(Georgia Department of Natural Resources, 2000), some of the lots in the neighborhood had only a 35 foot street frontage. Walking to the business district, people could chat with neighbors who tended the front yards or sat on ubiquitous front porches. Extended families sometimes lived in a block or in the neighborhood. Children who played on the sidewalk or walked to Washington Park had many eyes, often those of the elders in the community, keeping careful watch. Other African American communities replicated this type of space. Photographs of African American life document the behaviors nurtured in the slave landscape. For example, James Borchert's (1980) study, *Alley Life in Washington*, shows how people improvised courtyards in narrow alleys by placing chairs and sofas in the open for conversation and monitoring.

Beginning in 1999, I was a member of a research team investigating how children's experiences in social and physical spaces influenced behavioral and academic adjustment to school. In their home settings, we interviewed and observed parent/caregivers and first-grade children in a predominantly African American sample of Baltimore households. In poor but socially cohesive neighborhoods, where adults were likely to intervene in children's misbehavior, children had fewer behavior problems and positive school adjustment (Caughy, Nettles, & O'Campo, 2007). I was again reminded of the close, neighborly bonds of the Washington Park neighborhood, where grownups felt free to halt any child's inappropriate behavior or back talk (and tell parents what you did).

In our study, we coded videotaped tasks to examine connection between parent and child and its influence on behavior. When the pair showed mutual warmth and caring and mutual positive engagement, the child was less likely to show behavioral problems. But the physical aspects of the neighborhood made a difference in caregiver/child connectedness. Within a radius of up to six blocks of where a given child lived, observers rated the condition of buildings, amount and type of litter, and the condition of public spaces. When overall physical conditions were poor, caregivers in the videotapes engaged less in activities the child chose, less about feelings, and did not permit the child to ask questions.

*   *   *

Although my late uncle Ronald's wife and children still live in either the house on Desoto Street or in other houses in the Washington Park neighborhood, the multigenerational home ground that was present for most of my childhood exists only in my memory. Indeed, for many people, such spaces have vanished with increased mobility of the population, both within locales and beyond. The move to the suburbs has in particular broken the connection to generational space; I experienced this when my father moved us to a single-family home in Morrow, Georgia, in Clayton County. Ours was the first house on rural land undergoing development.

A new of form of generational space, "Children's Home" was the place that ChristopherAlexander and his colleagues (1977) envisioned for the network of learning. Such a place in each neighborhood would be where young children could be cared for without the parents for periods of a few hours or a few days. The home would be a communal space, one that supported children's needs for safety and interaction with adults and other children. Such arrangements, argued Alexander, "were absorbed in the large extended families of the past" where "the variety of adults and children of other ages had a positive value for the children" (Alexander et al., 1977, p. 427–428).

The play group, home daycare, and pre-kindergarten and after-school programs in the school building are the current arrangements that most resemble the "Children's Home." But child development research gives us glimpses into ways that culture is transmitted through imaginative encounters on home ground today. The literature on racial socialization, the transfer of information from adults to children regarding ethnicity and race, describes effective practices that have a positive impact on children's development. Exposing children to artifacts, music, art, and books—as well as conversing with children about cultural heroes and participating in cultural rituals and holidays—is an important part of child rearing that contributes to positive attitudes about their own group (Hughes et al., 2006). In one of the reports from our study just mentioned (Caughy, Nettles, O'Campo, & Lohrfink, 2006), the physical environment of the home gave us clues to how learning about African American heritage promotes positive outcomes for children. We found that when African American families had cultural artifacts, including photographs, in the home, their children had higher scores on tests of cognitive development than children whose homes were devoid of such objects. Remembering how our home overflowed with family photographs and books by African American authors, I was not surprised by this finding.

Connection—both to others and to places—is a foundational concern; we can seldom avoid its expression in human affairs and its representation in the sciences, the humanities, and the arts. Mindy Thompson Fullilove (1999) argues in *The House of Joshua: Meditations on Family and Place* that, "the sense of belonging to a locale" is the main consideration of a psychology of place. Indeed, various disciplines use the term "attachment" to describe relationships with other people, particularly primary caregivers, and to places. Connection can also refer to social support, a common way to examine how individuals form bonds to others. Social support is defined in many ways, including the presence or absence of interpersonal relationships; the frequency with which we make contact with others; and the extent to which we perceive and receive various types of support, such as emotional support, information, money, and time. Parents or other family members, as well as coaches and members, provide social resources for African American children (Nettles, Mucherah, & Jones, 2000).

In my case, Washington Park was not a community characterized by high incomes or vast wealth, though it certainly had more creature comforts than many other Atlanta communities or communities in rural Georgia. The neighborhood's significance to me lies in what it afforded: discovering my heritage and envisioning what I might become through connections with others across age, interests, and on home grounds of my extended kin. As Gundaker (1998) writes,

> African American home ground endures in the American landscape, from elite suburbs and tower apartments to the old homeplaces of the country-side, to the small table of family photos beside the bed of a housebound elder. Scale varies, but the claim, I am here, stays the same. (p. 3)

Notes

1. A recent transcription from the microfilm shows an "Elliett" Weems. Also, the Whites in the next household are shown with the surname "Winn," instead of Weems, with given names of "Rhos. D." and "Caroline." Retrieved from http://files.usgw.archives.net/ga/henry/census/1870/pg.0436.a.txt

2. Willow Hill School. Fisk University Rosenwald Card Database. Retrieved from http://www.rosenwald.fisk.edu/

3. In *Reflections in Black: A History of Black Photographers 1840 to the Present,* Deborah Willis (2000) writes that C. M. Battey (1873–1927) was among the photographers who "challenged the popular cultural myths concerning early-twentieth-century AfricanAmericans' visual culture" (p. 37). P. H. Polk, Addison Scurlock, Florestine Perrault Collins, James VanDerZee and Ellie Lee Weems were among the group who contributed to new images of African Americans.

2

Curriculum of Place

In her autobiography *Dust Tracks on a Road*, anthropologist and author Zora Neale Hurston (1891?–1960) describes her early years in Eatonville, Florida, a small town (population 600 at its peak) incorporated in 1889; Blacks owned the town and governed it. A 1920 map (Nathiri, 1991) shows the Hurston house one block from the Eatonville Elementary School, around the corner from the library and the St. Lawrence A. M. E. church, and one block down from the Odd Fellows Hall and the Joe Clarke Store. Hurston (1884) writes, "There were two churches, Methodist and Baptist, and the school. Most people would say that such institutions are always the great influences in any town. . . . But I know that Joe Clarke's store was the heart and spring of the town" (p. 61). In the store, she was introduced to folk tales about nature and spirits, and gossip about people in Eatonville. The customers and the men who "sat around" the store and its porch conveyed the lessons in language and story structure that had a part in Hurston's initiation as a writer. In "Figure and Fancy," the title of the chapter in which she describes this setting, Hurston alludes to how she began to design her own stories; she says, "When I began to make up stories I cannot say. Just from one fancy to another, adding more and more detail until they seemed real" (p. 70).

In other times and locales, economically diverse and segregated communities in the South gave African American children—like Hurston and me—access to many learning spaces. Here we found social support for being the persons we already were, and we rehearsed for roles we might undertake in the future. Such settings formed what Christopher Alexander and colleagues (1977) called "the network of learning: the thousands of interconnected situations that occur all over the city, and which in fact comprise the city's 'curriculum': the way of life it teaches to its young" (pp. 99–100).

By the late 1800s, much teaching and learning was formally anchored in schools and churches, although other places were physical sites for lessons beyond literacy, classics, and industrial trades. A child with trusting parents could access places in the network of learning (such as green spaces and the growing number of business places) with ease, alone or in the company of others. Historically, networks (such as those in cities like Charleston, Atlanta, and Richmond, and rural towns like Eatonville) provided the resources needed to support student investments of time and effort in schooling and also inspired and sustained children's dreams and aspirations. Adults in these places heeded W. E. B. Du Bois' advice in his 1920 essay, "The Immortal Child":

> Let us then return to fundamental ideals. Children must be trained in a knowledge of what the world is and what it knows and how it does its daily work. These things cannot be separated: we cannot teach pure knowledge apart from actual facts, or separate truth from the human mind. Above all we must not forget that the object of all education is the child itself and not what it does or makes. (p. 209)

The City

Charleston

Mamie Garvin Fields (1888–1987) writes of the power associated with freedom to explore. In *Lemon Swamp and Other Places: A Carolina Memoir* (1983), she describes Charleston at the end of the 19th century and the turn of the 20th century as a place with many spaces for learning. Some of these places were city landmarks (such as the Battery and Ft. Sumter), and some of them embedded in Black family life in the city (such as Miss Anna Eliza Izzard's School, built in the back of the parental home). Fields was born a few blocks away from the Battery, the park along the shores of the Charleston peninsula. When she was child, Blacks and Whites, although socially segregated, lived in close proximity. She writes, "Back then, we didn't have such a thing as an all-black 'inner-city.' That didn't come until very lately, since school desegregation.... black and white people lived uptown and they lived downtown, the black families among the white families, and vice versa" (pp. 18–19).

Recollecting adventures led by Miss Izzard (Fields' Cousin Lala), Fields described visits to various places around the city, including a treat at the ice cream shop: "So although we couldn't stop on the Battery or use the park, we visited it anyhow. We got our history lesson. We got our "sociology" lesson. And at the end we got our recreation. All that was Lala's doing" (1983, p. 55). Some of the history lessons were conducted on a street corner near the College of Charleston, where an older woman named "Aunt Jane" sold bread and sweets. "If you would stay," writes Fields, "she would tell you stories about her home 'cross the sea', and she would tell about our old folks right here in South Carolina" (p. 52). In her walks with Cousin Lala, and her writing about the Fourth of July, Fields tells of a day the Black people of Charleston gathered at the Battery. Whites shunned the Fourth as a Yankee holiday. "So the white people stayed home and the black people 'took over' the Battery for a day. The people were happy to be there, able to do what they felt like" (p. 56).

Fields' description of the experiences afforded by places in her network varied from setting to setting. When she talked about what she learned in the home, she told of her ancestral past. The adults in the three-generation household, including her Uncle J. B., a Methodist minister, told her stories about her forebears and how they were educated. Fields corresponded with Uncle J. B. when he traveled for the church. He took on the role of coach, correcting her grammar and urging her to rewrite and enliven the events she shared with him. She wrote to him frequently, practicing her writing and penmanship as well as her relational strength and efficacy.

In her home, Fields learned about physical differences within her own family. She and her brother were the brownest of four siblings, one boy and three girls: "When my sister Hattie was born, the people came from all around to see her, because she was so light and had gray eyes and brown hair" (1983, p. 47). Early on, she learned that lighter-skinned Black people were privileged: "When I was a little girl, I recognized that there was a difference, because my brother Herbert used to tease me and call me black—'blackymo'.... He would say, 'Well, we are the black ones and they are the light ones. They can do this and that.'" (p. 47). Fields described other incidents that showed ways of equating color with status within the African American community that did not violate her sense of worth. She preferred, for instance, not to attend a private African American high school that gave honors only to lighter-toned children and to mulattos. She commented, "It didn't matter what you did if you were dark. Used to leading my class up to elementary school, I hated this idea, so I began to say I wanted to go somewhere else" (p. 47).

Scholars did not begin empirical studies of racial consciousness among African American children until the 1930s, when psychologists Kenneth and Mamie Clark (1939) initiated a research program on racial identity and preferences. One of the most widely known of the Clarks' findings (and used in the 1954 *Brown v. Board of Education* case) was that African American preschool children frequently preferred and expressed positive attitudes toward White, rather than Brown or Black dolls (Clark & Clark, 1947). Later, Margaret Beale Spencer, a developmental psychologist, showed that such racial preferences can be distinct from children's self-concepts, that is, children can have positive attitudes about themselves as well as expressing a preference for light-skin tones (Swanson, Cunningham, Youngblood, & Spencer, 2009).

On her city block, Fields experienced how Jim Crow divided Blacks and Whites. Her family was close to a German family, the Eyes, who lived across the street. The children played together outside, and occasionally the families borrowed small supplies, such as sugar and coffee, from each other. Those cordial relations changed as Jim Crow laws became increasingly severe. Jim Crow affected all relations between the two families. The children used marbles as weapons instead of playing with them on the ground. Name calling ensued: the Black children called the White children "crackers," and the White children called the Black children "niggers." The Eyes had a store adjacent to their house, which closed because Black families no longer bought their goods there. Fields writes,

> For long years after Jim Crow, the Eyes stayed in that house across the street from us. Right there, for years and years, although Charleston life was as segregated as you please. The law made it that we weren't really neighbors anymore. We didn't have anything to do with each other, although we still knew each other from a distance. (1983, p. 49)

Fields learned that the girls in the family became teachers and married. "We went on, too. I became a teacher, married, and had my children" (p. 49).

Jacksonville

Mamie Garvin Fields was 34 in 1923, when my mother was born in Charleston. Edna Lewis (shown in Figure 2.1) was the sixth of seven children born to Emmaline Turner Lewis (1887–1954), an accomplished seamstress, and Eugene Richard Lewis (1885–1951), a chief railway postal clerk on the Atlantic Coast Line.[1] Grandmother Lewis attended a private sewing school and learned to read patterns rather than guessing how to construct a garment. My grandfather's heritage was Gullah/Geechee, descendants of enslaved people whose original homes were in west and central Africa. Africans brought knowledge of rice, cotton, and indigo cultivation to plantations along the coasts of the Carolinas, Georgia, and Florida, and made critical contributions to the North American plantation economy (Gomez, 1998). The Gullah/Geechee people have their own linguistic traditions; my mother recalls that she had trouble understanding my grandfather when he spoke. She remembers little of her time in Charleston, save for the name of the street where the family lived and the name of her church. The family moved to Jacksonville when she was 2 or 3 years old. Her father's route had changed, and he was given the choice of moving to Washington, DC, or to Jacksonville. He chose the latter, perhaps because the city, like Charleston, had a sizable Gullah/Geechee population.[2]

Figure 2.1 Edna Lewis in Jacksonville, Florida, ca. 1930. *Source:* Personal collection of Edna Lewis Rice.

In Jacksonville, my grandfather bought a new, seven-room house on Davis Street. The kitchen had a cookstove and an electric stove. With a second income from Grandmother Lewis's skills as a seamstress, the family weathered the Depression. All of the children attended historically Black colleges and universities and subsequently entered professions that afforded middle-class lifestyles. In my mother's first year of college, she met my father in Jacksonville, at Uncle Ellie Weems's photography studio. They courted throughout college (he was at Morehouse, she at Bennett); they married after she graduated and they settled in Atlanta.

As children, my mother and her siblings seldom had an idle moment. In addition to all of them learning to play musical instruments, "We all had to work with our hands." In the home, my mother learned to sew, knit, crochet, and cane chairs. (One of her legacies is a large number of crocheted throws, one for each of her children, grandchildren, and friends.) Beyond the home, learning places for the Lewis children were school (Mom attended Davis Street Elementary from the first to the eighth grade); the public library, to which they walked once a week (the family had only one bicycle for the seven children); and church. My mother said, "There were no parks (we played in the yard); no recreation, no YWCA." During the summers, the family went to Fernandina,[3] "the only beach we could go to. We would go out early Saturday or Sunday morning and come back late in the evening. We would take our own food."

She observed her father practicing for the tests he had to take for promotion in his job. "In his bedroom, he had a scheme, a box he built for sorting mail. The box had a slot for each city on his rail postal route. He practiced sorting with index cards. His job was a government job; he made $700 a month, which was high pay for a Negro man." In part, her memories coincide with the Federal Writer's Project description of the Depression years in Jacksonville's Black community (McDonogh, 1993). The number of Black workers decreased greatly during the economic downturn, but even when employment was high, three categories predominated for males: agriculture, domestic work (including tourism), and commerce. Women's work tended to be domestic and in factories and laundries. Housing conditions in the state were often poor. In Jacksonville, a federal low-cost housing project (Durkeville), replaced unsanitary and crowded housing in 1937. The Florida Tennis Association and the Lincoln Golf Club in Jacksonville were popular outlets and two of the few examples of structured leisure activities. My mother recalled that her father taught each of his children to play tennis on the segregated courts.

I sensed from my mother's description that her parents were authoritarian: they had strict rules, and they expected the children to obey. Viewed in the context of the times, my grandparents are understandable. How could parents be assured that their children would not question White authority if they did not respect parents in their own home? Above all, my grandparents sought respectability for the family.

There was political organizing within Jacksonville's Black community during the 1920s and 1930s. For example, the Masonic Temple, designed in 1913, was a place where Black community leaders met to consider politics and business (African American Historic Places, 1994). Moreover, Jacksonville had many African American social and improvement societies. But the Lewis family kept to themselves and did not participate in politics; according to my mother

> ...we knew what was going on, but we weren't a political family. There was too much lynching. You couldn't do a thing about it. My father carried a gun with him when he went to work. You talked in your house and what you talked about stayed in the house.

Despite the family's apparent reluctance to speak out about their fears, my grandfather Lewis gives us a clue as to how, in the face of racial oppression, his efforts were trained to a singular focus. He often recited his aim in life; my mother recalled it verbatim: "to rear his children so they wouldn't have to work in a White woman's kitchen or a White man's yard."

Atlanta

"Thinking like a free person was not easy for a black child growing up in the South in the 1930s and 1940s," writes James H. Cone (1991) in describing the Atlanta childhood of Martin Luther King Jr., 6 years younger than my father, George H. Rice Sr. (Figure 2.2). He also grew up in Atlanta. Despite the age differences and the places they called home (King's home was in East Atlanta, and my father lived in the westside neighborhood of Washington Park), there were some similarities in their everyday lives. Both of their fathers grew up on farms not far from each other: King Sr. in Stockbridge, Georgia, and George E. Rice in Ellenwood, about 15 miles away. Both fathers had gone to Morehouse; both families were Baptist.

Church and home were the most important contexts in King's life, according to Cone (1991). Church also played a role as a learning space in my father's life; he attended his family's church, Friendship Baptist. About a mile from the Washington Park neighborhood, the refurbished ivory stucco church, founded in 1866, stands in its original location near the Georgia Dome in downtown Atlanta. During my father's boyhood, the Reverend Maynard Jackson, father of Atlanta's first Black mayor, led religious services

Figure 2.2   Ellie L. Weems. George H. Rice, Sr. and father, George E. Rice, ca. 1931. *Source:* Personal collection of Saundra Rice Murray Nettles.

for church members and visitors, social and medical services for the poor families who lived in the immediate vicinity of the church, and youth services for children in the neighborhood and the membership. The 85th Anniversary program (Friendship Baptist Church, n.d.) includes the elaborate organizational chart of the church's religious offerings and its outreach to the impoverished community in which the church was located (Figure 2.3). The adjacent brick building, demolished when I was a child, had housed medical services, a credit union, and meeting rooms. Articles in the *Atlanta Daily World*, at the time the only daily African American newspaper in the

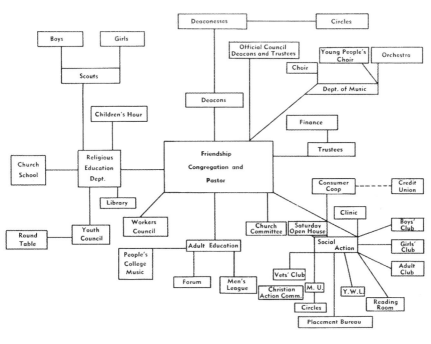

Figure 2.3   Organization chart, c. 1951. *Source:* Friendship Baptist Church, 85th Anniversary.

United States, show that my father was a junior assistant scoutmaster in Troop 95 of the Boy Scouts at Friendship (High School Boasts, 1939). In late childhood and early adolescence, he had mastered several skills required for merit badges in Troop 90 at the First Congregational Church (Scout Promotions, 1933; Several Local Boy Scouts, 1936).[4]

Home provided learning opportunities for George Rice. I grew up in the same house and found evidence in the home environment. Bookshelves lined the stairs to the basement; my grandmother saved many of the textbooks, novels, and reference books her children had used. When I was a child, I could look up homework in an old edition of the *Encyclopedia Britannica* (my parents would later buy a current edition for us); read *Gone with the Wind*, *Invisible Man*, and *Annie Allen*; and browse through the Boy Scout handbooks when I was a Girl Scout.

Outdoor Spaces in Urban and Rural Areas

But nature was also an important environment for George Rice. While their mother worked as a domestic in Atlanta during the summers, George and his four siblings (three sisters and one brother) went to their grandparents' farm in Henry County, Georgia. He knew the rural house so well that he drew it for me, including details such as the arrangement of furniture. One of his chores was helping his grandfather earn money from crops. My mother told me, "He used to ride with granddaddy in his wagon to a farmer's market near Atlanta. They sold peaches, watermelons, and corn." His love of natural surroundings, farming, and animal care would continue for the rest of his life. As an adult, he moved our family to a rural area, planted tomatoes, lima beans, and other vegetables, and, for a brief period, had horses. He never wrote about his feelings for the natural world, but I recall a painting he did when he was a young boy. It hung in a hallway of our house and depicted, serene and still, a forest, a lake, and a boat.

Fields (1983) and Hurston (1942) wrote extensively about their experiences in nature. Fields associated her grandfather's South Carolina farm with varied experiences. She called one of the many swamps, Lemon Swamp, a "special treat" to enter:

> Riding in, you felt like you were going into a room. Even at midday, when the sun burned down very bright, the light was dim inside. Trees and bushes threw shadows across the water and the ground. Those were like the curtains of the room. (p. 67)

Her favorite cousin taught her to drive a wagon and mule and "how to run down a chicken and pluck it; how to pick the vegetables without hurting the plant" (p. 70). Hurston wrote,

> I was only happy in the woods, and when the ecstatic Florida springtime came strolling from the sea, trance-glorifying the world with its aura. I nibbled sweet oat stalks and listened to the wind sloughing and sighing through the crowns of the lofty pines. I made particular friendship with one high tree and always played about its roots. (p. 56)

Journalist Charlayne Hunter-Gault, in her memoir *In My Place*, recalled her experiences out-of-doors, in yards and other natural landscapes of the rural South. For example, she described a space for renewal through play in Covington, Georgia, one of the places she lived when she was a child. Next to her house was an empty lot "that made an excellent, albeit barren, playground for me and the many children in the neighborhood" (1992, p. 32). A mulberry tree grew on the lot, and she wrote, "I climbed it often, feeling that its upper branches, high above the ground I knew so well, held out the promise of revealing the old tree's secrets" (p. 32).

Contemporary research on child development and natural settings confirms and extends intuitive notions that children benefit from contact with nature. Children find nature restorative, prefer to be outdoors (especially in natural settings), show reduced symptoms of ADHD after playing in nature (Evans, 2006), and often have special places such as houses made of leafy branches and secret dens in wooded areas (Sobel, 2002). In one study, Andrea Faber Taylor and her colleagues (Taylor, Wiley, & Kuo, 1998) observed African American children, ages 3 to 12, at play in the Ida B. Wells Homes, a public housing project (now demolished) in Chicago. In green spaces (those with trees and other vegetation), children played more and engaged in more creative play than children did in areas with sparse greenery. While the majority of the children had adult supervision, children in green spaces had more access to adults than they had in barren spaces. Recently, the Tuskegee University's Youth Garden Project (McArthur, Hill, Trammel, & Morris, 2010) engaged African American children (ages 5 through 13) who lived in public housing. With the support of college student mentors, the children planted, harvested, and marketed different crops on plots located at the Tuskegee Agricultural Experiment Station. The children reported that the project was fun and that they wanted to garden at home. Children showed positive social and pro-nature behavior, and their grades improved.

*   *   *

For me, my favorite place was the park, the first recreational facility for African Americans in Atlanta, and like for Hurston, a space to explore. The park was named Washington Park and was only a block from our house on Desoto Street (Figure 2.4).

The park had two pools. One, the swimming pool, was more oval than round, and you could look down on it from the wire fence lining the stone pathway on the wooded hill that protected the southern and eastern sides. To the north stood the pool house, a wooden structure with a ticket office that separated the locker rooms for males and females. The deep end was to the west, ringed by a concrete plaza. The pool in Washington Park was the only public place in Atlanta in which African Americans could swim.

Every chance I had, my sister and I and other children would sneak over to the other pool. "Don't go near the creek," the grownups routinely warned when we children got permission to explore the park all by ourselves. Dirty water (at 8 years old or so, I had not heard of pollution or worse, sewerage) trickled from a concrete pipe, say 9 or 10 feet in diameter, slightly rough to the touch and to my eye, so perfect a form that we could

Figure 2.4   Ronald W. Bailey. View of Washington Park from Desoto Street, 2006.

climb to its top, which was wide enough for us to walk on and peer over the edge into the slender stream that disappeared into the silt at its edge. A hilly area rose from the bank opposite where we usually stood before we climbed, and on its summit, tucked in the weeds and scraggly trees, was a shack, burned black, rotting one or two crisp splinters at a time. At the time, it was the ultimate discovery place: secluded, challenging, and mysterious. We (my sister or a cousin, sometimes a friend) asked questions and made up answers. Who had lived in the shack? (A bum, a family of ghosts, slaves.) Why and when did it burn? (Indians, maybe even pilgrims, whose campfire burned out of control.) What in the dirty water was so bad that grownups forbade us to explore?

We would linger only a few minutes at the creek. We did not want to risk being found there, so we would run into a large playing field to see what was going on—usually football or baseball—and then count each step on a short flight up another hill where the tennis courts were. Except for lessons, kids did not get on the courts to play much. I would pause to admire the pleated white tennis dresses that elegant women wore and watch for trains to come on the tracks that ran parallel to the courts. Then I would head for the playground at the southeastern-most tip of the park, where the biggest attraction was yet another staircase, made of silver-painted iron, leading to the top of the bar from which swings were attached. A slide would have completed the journey down, but for many summers, the steps led nowhere. I would climb them anyway (if grownups weren't around) and pretend that I was perhaps Captain Hook on the lookout for ships at sea. Then the sandbox beckoned, with silicon grains that could be piled and patted into castles and Eskimo huts.

* * *

My freedom to roam the gentle hills of Washington Park resembles thoughts that W. E. B. Du Bois had had about his native western Massachusetts. In *Dusk of Dawn: An Essay Toward an Autobiography of a Race Concept* (1940), he writes,

> Meanwhile the town and its surroundings were a boy's paradise: there were mountains to climb and rivers to wade and swim; lakes to freeze and hills for coasting. There were orchards and caves and wide green fields; and all of it was apparently property of the children of the town. (p. 13)

Du Bois himself was connected to west Atlanta through his work as a professor of sociology at Atlanta University Center, located east of the Washington Park neighborhood business district.

Booker T. Washington (1856–1915), however, writes of a fearful experience of nature in *Up From Slavery: An Autobiography* (1901). He tells of going to the mill on the plantation where he grew up, a journey fraught with fearful anticipation: that the loaded bag of corn would slop from the horse's back and that he would fall with it and have to stand hours waiting for rescue:

> The road was a lonely one, and often led through dense forests. I was always frightened. The woods were said to be full of soldiers who had deserted from the army, and I had been told that the first thing a deserter did to a Negro boy when he found him alone was to cut off his ears. Besides, when I was late in getting home I knew I would always get a severe scolding or a flogging. (p. 6)

Later, after Emancipation, he similarly dreaded the salt-furnaces and coal mines of Virginia. Cleanliness came hard, and access to schooling, which he desired above all, was thwarted as his work in the mines was a necessary contribution to the family's survival.

Scholars often contrast the racial ideologies of Du Bois and Washington; the poet Dudley Randall (1914–2000) captured the essence of disagreements between the two in the poem entitled, "Booker T. and W. E. B." (Randall, 1969). The first two verses depict Washington arguing in favor of industrial arts, opposed to the study of liberal arts, which Du Bois advocated. The second two verses contrast the men's views on civil rights, with Washington admonishing Blacks to refrain from complaints while Du Bois, co-founder of the NAACP and ardent leader in the Black freedom struggle, argues for "dignity and justice." The poem ends, neither man compromising.

> "It seems to me, said Booker T.—
> "I don't agree,"
> Said W.E.B.

Perhaps their differing views are rooted literally in the very grounds of their childhood: for Du Bois, the natural field of thought roaming unfettered over vast expanses, contemplating principled causes, and by contrast for Washington, the landscape of hardship and necessity.

Like Washington, writer Richard Wright's childhood was rife with adversity. Wright (1908–1960) tells us in *Black Boy* (2005) about the experience of nearly burning down his family's home when he 4 years old, experimenting with fire. After his mother punished him, he had visions so terrifying that he could barely sleep. As he recovers, he finds,

> Each event spoke with a cryptic tongue. And the moments of living slowly revealed their coded meanings. There was the wonder I felt when I first saw a brace of mountainlike, spotted, black-and-white horses clopping down a dusty road through clouds of powdered clay. (p. 7)

And he ends, "There was the cloudy notion of hunger when I breathed the odor of new-cut, bleeding grass. And there was the quiet terror that suffused my senses when vast hazes of gold washed earthward from star-heavy skies on silent nights" (p. 9). When he was 5, Wright's impoverished parents moved the family from Natchez to Memphis, where they lived in a one-story brick tenement house. This would be the first of the moves Wright describes. In Memphis, he writes, "The absence of green, growing things made the city seem dead" (p. 10). In descriptions of his childhood, Wright takes the rich, sensory world and creates politically charged literature, evoking the human capacity to embrace nature.

Places of Business

Black enterprise in the United States evolved from enslaved persons whose masters permitted them to hire out their own time after their daily work and from free persons who served Whites and Blacks as barbers, grocers, blacksmiths, shoemakers, carpenters, and undertakers. In some cases, business, such as dressmaking, was conducted in the home, and in other cases, in shops. The construction of buildings to house a diverse array of entrepreneurial ventures intensified after the Civil War. In "Mapping the Terrain of Black Richmond," Elsa Barkley Brown and Gregg D. Kimball (1995) tell us, "In the immediate post-Civil War era, black Richmonders erected buildings that tangibly testified to their emancipation" (p. 314). As in other cities, African Americans built churches, schools, and businesses such as banks, stores, and theaters. According to Meier and Lewis (1959), social and economic conditions changed dramatically at the turn of the 20th century. Whites became less likely to deal with Black entrepreneurs, and the influx of Blacks from rural areas into the cities created a Negro clientele in need of goods and services. In Memphis, where Wright's family moved in 1913, Beale Street was a major African American business district—as the home of W. C. Handy and the blues, the site of Ida B. Wells' paper (*Free Speech*) as well as saloons, restaurants, the Tri-State Bank building, and the Palace Theater (African American Historic Places, 1994; Chase, 1994). But Wright does not give us details of the location of his home or its surrounds.

At 6, before his mother enrolled him in school, Wright attempted to read by questioning students about the contents of books they left on the sidewalk when they stopped to play on the way home. He learned to count from the man who delivered coal to his house, and after that, his mother taught him to read and told him stories. But some lessons were less desirable. He writes, "I was a drunkard in my sixth year, before I had begun school. With a gang of children, I roamed the streets, begging pennies from passers-by, haunting the doors of saloons, wandering farther and farther away from home each day" (2005, p. 21). His mother beat him, prayed for him, cried for him. She enlisted an elderly Black woman to keep him at home while she worked. "The craving for alcohol finally left me and I forgot the taste of it" (p. 22).

In Atlanta, "Sweet Auburn" Avenue was the most prominent business district, but Washington Park had its own small businesses on the streets named Hunter (now Martin Luther King Avenue) and Ashby (now Joseph E. Lowery Boulevard). I remember Hunter Street as the route the Washington High School Band took when it led the Homecoming Parade. The high school band would pass the William A. Harris Memorial Hospital, the first private Negro hospital in Atlanta. Dr. Charles William Powell established the 30-bed hospital in 1928 to perform surgery, which municipal and White-owned hospitals forbade Black doctors to do (Journal of the National Medical Association, 1939). On holidays, our Girl Scout troop visited children who were patients there, and my family would call on relatives. The hospital was a few doors away from the Ashby Theatre, where my friends and I would join other kids for Saturday matinees. I shopped with my mother at the grocery store and fish market on Ashby Street and spent many hours at the beauty shops on Hunter Street. We ate at Paschal Brothers Restaurant, site of many meetings during the Civil Rights Movement. Now, one of its concessions is a customer favorite at the Atlanta Hartsfield/Jackson International Airport.

Architect Sharon Sutton maintains that what children learn from their real and virtual surroundings is filtered by race and social class. She writes,

> Public space teaches children their roles in society. Since young children have minimally refined language and belief systems, it seems logical that a primary source of their knowledge comes through direct experience of their physical and social milieu, the former limiting or promoting certain types of activities and exchanges, that, in turn, influence what is learned and from whom. These direct observations are elaborated by the language and attitudes assimilated from significant others to form children's views of who they are, and who they can become. (1996, p. 2)

I did not have to imagine a person of color in a white lab coat. I saw a Black pharmacist when my mother took me to Amos Drug Store. With its selection of magazines, jewelry, and cherry Cokes, it was my favorite business. My family and neighbors interacted with Black restaurant owners (male and female), photographers, bank tellers, barbers, gas station owners, dentists, and doctors. The facilities were substantial, one- or two-story brick buildings, their interiors, to my child's eye, clean and plain.

Moreover, Washington Park was what is now called a "walkable" neighborhood—a safe neighborhood in which people live near desired destinations (schools, work, stores, and churches), streets are linked, and children can actively commute to schools by walking or biking.[5] Beyond walkability, we children heard our parents speak with pride about the advances that Negroes (as we called ourselves then) had made, symbolized by the neat homes, well-maintained yards, civic participation as voters and volunteers in community institutions (such as churches, fraternities and sororities, and schools), and businesses that could hire our own when others would not. Televisions were rare; we read, skated, and played rock school for amusement. Although our parents patronized some White establishments on occasion, there we found frequent "Whites Only" signs. Looking back at the African American places of business, I see an empowered community. Owners were models of self-efficacy; their businesses were symbols of the owners' sense of responsibility to the economically viable community.

Nearby Neighborhood Places

City Blocks: Atlanta and Richmond in Mid-Century

Our city block in Atlanta's Washington Park neighborhood was the learning landscape of my early school years, where my friends and I could walk, solo or in groups, to different places without adult supervision. You could take a brisk walk around the entire block, including Ollie Street, facing the neighborhood park, in about 20 minutes. As a child (I was 5 years old in 1952), I could start at my house, go to the right past a duplex and seven houses (including one whose owner had a horse living in a backyard shed), cut through the elementary school playground to Lena Street with eight or nine houses and the neighborhood store, and skip past three houses on Ollie Street. Timing depended on the task. Selling candy for curtains in the school auditorium was a good hour. And 15 minutes would suffice when I was avoiding a yard where I'd been scolded one day for picking irresistible, gorgeous flowers. "They're for everybody to enjoy," said the owner, an elderly, brown-skinned lady who wore a flowered house dress and hairnet covering her grayed hair. "If I catch you doing it again, I'll tell your grandmamma," she warned.

*   *   *

On a cool June night, the grownups who lived in our house on Desoto Street—grandmamma and Papa, mama and daddy, Uncle Ronald—sat on the front porch in metal chairs whose shell-shaped backs were painted a new color each summer. This particular summer, in the mid50s, they were pale green. We children fidgeted on the gray steps that led from the porch to a cement landing, a white square edged in yellow fieldstone. There were seven steps, just enough for promotions from first to the seventh grade in games of rock school. That night, the grownups urged us to organize a game—anything to keep us from running back and forth from the stairs to the sidewalk and asking, "When's it coming? When's it coming?" Someone, perhaps Pat (my younger sister), or Melma Jean (our friend from around the corner), yelled out, "Look!" It was twilight—just before the street lights were turned on—and we knew if we moved quickly enough we would see the start of our neighborhood's Lantern Parade.

We bolted to the sidewalk and looked up Desoto Street. From the playground at the school on our block, past Mr. Gretcham's house and Mr. Smith's house were the first marchers. They walked in the glow of lanterns, handmade by the marchers, of cardboard boxes whose sides had been cut away and filled with crepe paper. Some lanterns had silhouettes of characters from fairy tales. The most elaborate was Cinderella's pumpkin, so large it was mounted on a wagon. Inside the lanterns, candles burned. Today the lanterns would be deemed a fire hazard, but I don't recall any that any ever caught fire.

The marchers walked quietly past our house to Washington Park. We left the porch with our parents, taking a shortcut through the park to the playing field where the marchers were assembling. They extinguished the candles, the field lights came up to cheers, and the marchers performed a program of dances from all over the world.

Atlanta's Parks and Recreation Department organized this annual event (Martin, 1987). The summer when I participated, I made my lantern and practiced my dance at "the hut," a one-room cinderblock building in a corner of the playground of our neighborhood school. Miss Daniels, who led the construction of the lanterns and other activities, was always present when the hut was open. I don't recall that she had helpers. She seemed tall to me, but that was from my child's-eye view, and wore white blouses on her medium-sized frame. Her voice was pleasant and warm; it warbled when she led us in songs from *Snow White and the Seven Dwarfs, Cinderella,* and other Disney songs on colorful 45 rpm vinyl disks. She acted out scenes from fairy tales and applauded at our little dances.

I went to the hut with my sister Pat and two of our friends from Desoto Street, sometimes on Saturdays and many days in the summer. One summer, Miss Daniels taught us the *jota,* a Spanish dance, and American square dances at a summer program at B. T. Washington High School, two blocks away from Desoto Street. During that summer of the recreational program, I had one class, home economics, in the building. I felt very grown-up as I went from the gym and the dance classes to the floor where the home economics room was. On the way, I would pass large murals on the main hall opposite the front doors. I was fascinated with the scenes of people working; they seemed to be all angles in muted colors of clay, green, and blue. As an adult, I learned that the murals were painted by the father of my psychology professor at Howard. Wilmer Jennings, the artist, was a student when he created the murals in 1928 in a style that resembles works of WPA artists.

Although my mother took my sister and me to summer daycamp and other children's programs at the Phyllis Wheatley Branch of the YWCA, the humble hut was the locus of my recreational life—the enrichment part, the arts part as we acted out fairy tales and made objects out of cardboard, crepe paper, and clay; the social learning part that came with games of hopscotch, jackstones, and Old Maid; the "multicultural" part that we learned through dances of other people and places; the discipline we learned as we practiced for the dances that concluded the lantern parade.

* * *

The hut was on the grounds of E. R. Carter Elementary School, which my father attended in the 1920s and 1930s. Known as the Ashby Street School when it had been built for White students in 1910, the school had been renamed for the Reverend Edward Randolph Carter, who was once the minister of our church, Friendship Baptist Church. Journalist Charlayne Hunter-Gault, who attended the school in the early 1950s, wrote in her 1992 memoir, *In My Place*, "Attending a school named for a Black person was part of the way in which Black history was celebrated and passed on every day, as opposed to just one month out of the year" (p. 75). Explaining that that Black schools had to teach Black history, although the textbooks ignored this aspect of United States history, Black teachers "could prepare us through the power they knew no one could deny them: the transmission of a heritage that we could be proud of and inspired by" (p. 75). When I look back, I can see, as Hunter-Gault did, that Black history so permeated my everyday life that no extraordinary markers were necessary.

My favorite teacher, Miss Fields, taught me in the third and fourth grades. She was the person who introduced my classmates and me to events beyond our neighborhood, to ways of relating to others, and to possibilities and talents that lay within us. She prepared our class for trips to hear the Atlanta Symphony Orchestra's concerts for young people. With the city auditorium filled with Black children, *Peter and the Wolf* sounded the same way as it did when I listened to Leonard Bernstein's *Young People's Concerts* on television. I learned that home-school relations could be coordinated; she and my father, a mathematics teacher at Booker T. Washington High, both taught me arithmetic. But I'd been unable to reconcile their two distinct approaches; and Miss Fields had noticed my distress. The two of them worked out a joint approach: Miss Fields would introduce me to arithmetic while my father tutored me after school and saw to it that I completed my homework. But best of all, Miss Fields encouraged me to practice—not only arithmetic and reading, but writing plays and directing my classmates in them, even though the pieces seldom had proper midpoints and few had cathartic moments. I learned that practice, not impossible adult standards, counted.

* * *

Every Saturday afternoon, I walked around Ollie Street to Lena Street, turned the corner, and rang the bell at the first house, although I was always tempted to go to the building next to it, The Store. The Store was as close to a cabin shack as one could get in the city. Quite small with a single counter and shelves with bread, milk, chips, and candy, The Store was the place in which I learned to make change, ask for exactly what I wanted to purchase, and otherwise behave as a proper consumer should. One of the two White men I encountered regularly in my childhood owned and operated the small enterprise. (The other was my father's employer, Mr. Ludy, a photographer for whom he worked part-time.) The Store was directly behind our house on Desoto Street, and we children could cut through the backyard, open the gate, and approach the back of The Store via a narrow path in a weed-filled lot.

But I could not dally at The Store, be late to Mr. Sullivan's house, where he taught piano lessons to children in the neighborhood. The small house smelled to me like a mixture of dust, camphor, and moth balls. The piano, a spinet, stood in a corner of the tiny living room next to wall. Mr. Sullivan had a metronome, which he seldom used, preferring to tap the time with a pencil against the ledge above the keyboard when he wasn't tapping our fingers with the pencil. On the wall next to the piano hung a framed cartoon that depicted a large, bum-like man in ragged clothes, lecturing to a nonexistent audience. The words read, "If you're so smart, how come you ain't rich?" Waiting for a lesson, I amused myself by reading and reflecting upon "rich" and who or what it signified. Certainly I noticed differences about things in people's home and made inferences: my father told a story about how I, as a 3 year old, responded to my great aunt Mae when she told me that she and my uncle had no milk, cookies, or ice cream in their home. They had no children, and Aunt Mae was a public health nurse who, in her daily work, coached Black families on the importance of healthy food choices. My father reported that I exclaimed, "You must be poor." (I learned later that they were my most affluent relatives, but snack food was the signifier for me.)

Activist Randall Robinson, in his 1999 memoir, *Defending the Spirit: A Black Life in America*, reveals a similar reaction to things in his Richmond, Virginia, home:

Unlike the dangling strings at home, Grandma and Granddaddy had light switches on the wall with two buttons in a toggle plate.... This was the first place I had ever seen such a switch, and I was very impressed. I thought Grandma and Granddaddy must have been rich. (p. 25)

Robinson gives a detailed portrait of his Richmond block in the 1940s and 1950s: the high school principal and his family lived in one side of a duplex around the corner; two prostitutes lived across the street from Robinson's family; the "flamboyant owner" of a gas station lived nearby. He "drove a fire engine red Hudson convertible. He put his Christmas tree up on his front porch in November and took it down in March" (p. 15–16). Other neighbors were Shirley's Beauty Parlor and his uncle Charles, a physician who treated poor Blacks. Robinson writes, "On our block segregation compelled what would otherwise have been a very unlikely black unity" (p. 15).

Research on how children notice social class is limited, but Heather Johnson and Margaret Hagerman (2006) review studies that show that children as young as 6 are aware of differences in social class, preschool children can recognize attributes of rich and poor people, and children, regardless of their own social class, recognize economic inequality.

Libraries

In her New York apartment, specifically in the kitchen, Paule Marshall's origins as a writer began. As a child in the 1930s, Marshall would sit quietly as she listened to women domestics who gathered at the table in her mother's house. Their talk ranged from gossip, to their native Barbados, to their new homes in America. Marshall (2001) writes that these women had a strong need for self-expression, "and since language was the only vehicle readily available to them they made of it an art form that—in keeping with the African tradition in which art and life are one—was an integral part of their lives" (p. 629).

Marshall viewed the women's talk as therapy, a reaffirmation of self-worth, and weapons against their feelings of invisibility and powerlessness. The kitchen table talk gave her frequent experiences of empowerment. The women's talk also gave her lessons in African sounds in the language and rhythm that the women themselves made as they pleased. But, Marshall says, "By the time I was 8 or 9, I graduated from the corner of the kitchen to the neighborhood library, and thus from the spoken to the written word" (p. 631). Reading the works of Paul Laurence Dunbar, born in 1872 to a couple who escaped from enslavement in Kentucky, Marshall imaginatively entered into words that healed, that aroused feelings of hope of romantic love and longing in the face of her separation from her father. Reading Dunbar, Marshall experienced both empowerment and connection. "Dunbar—his dark, eloquent face, his large volume of poems—permitted me to dream that I might someday write, and with something of the power with words my mother and her friends possessed" (p. 633).

In Atlanta, librarian Annie L. McPheeters (1908–1994) would provide similar opportunities for young Black people to experience the writings of Black authors. She gives us the facts about her early career in her 1988 memoir, *Library Service in Black and White*. In 1934, the Atlanta Public Library appointed her as Assistant Branch Librarian at the Auburn Avenue Branch. Opening in 1921, Auburn Avenue was the first branch library for Blacks in the city, and McPheeters was the first professional librarian in the system, having earned a Bachelor of Science in Library Science from Hampton Institute in Virginia. McPheeters led the effort to establish a Black History collection, which included works by Alain Locke, founder of the New Negro movement associated with the Harlem Renaissance, and W. E. B. Du Bois, who in 1902 had organized a committee of Blacks, demanding representation for Blacks on Atlanta's Library Board. Their demand was rejected, as were requests that Blacks be permitted to use the Carnegie Library, which opened to the public in 1902.

Mrs. McPheeters brought to her posts a special interest in the development of children and young people.[6] For preschoolers there were "read aloud" times (with mothers and older siblings serving as storytellers and readers); story hours in the library and on the radio; book reviews and discussion groups for young people; and The Puppeteers, students who made puppets and performed with an art instructor from the public schools. In her memoir (1988), she named my father as one of the members who told stories and worked the hand puppets on a stage.

* * *

When the West Hunter Branch library in Atlanta was dedicated in 1949, Mrs. McPheeters left the Auburn Avenue library to head the new branch. When I was old enough to walk there on my own, I went several times a week. At the library, my sister, brother, and I, as well as our friends, practiced reading and listening skills that first our parents, and later our teachers, had nurtured. We read Black authors and participated in the Summer Reading Club.

My nose told me I was there. The vestibule of West Hunter Branch library had a rubbery smell, like new tires, perhaps from the tiles that lined the entrance. I would stand for a minute in the reception area while the plate glass doors closed behind me. Stepping into another world requires a little ritual of anticipation—a few deep breaths and I was ready to open the door to the circulation and lounge areas to the right and the children's area to the left. The adult space was straight ahead.

I always looked for Mrs. McPheeters. Her presence, like a fresh, light perfume, filled the library (and, I am told, years after her death, her spirit is still there). Her body emanated agency—you could sense that she had just shelved a stray book left on a table, or realigned a chair. The reading rooms were quiet, Zen spaces where a child could close her eyes, one hand resting on the page just read, and follow the character into the life that beckoned from pictures and words.

When she was around, I trained my eyes and ears in her direction. When she read books during story hours (Figure 2.5), I listened to the rise and fall of her voice while watching how she moved her hand when she turned the pages. I saw how she listened and nodded and asked questions when I summarized the contents of books I had read for Vacation Reading

Figure 2.5   West Hunter Branch Story Hour with Mrs. A. L. McPheeters. *Source:* Annie L. McPheeters Collection, Archives Division, Auburn Avenue Research Library on African American Culture and History, Atlanta-Fulton Public Library System.

Club. I overheard her when she told my mother I had read virtually every book in the children's section and was ready to read (selectively and under her guidance) books in the adult section. She coached another child and me in diction and expression as we rehearsed the poetry of Langston Hughes. I remembered her instructions and followed them when we taped a broadcast for the Black radio station, WERD. Even when she performed the simple task of checking out books, using a date stamp attached to a pencil, I observed how precisely she kept within the lines of the date due slip glued inside the back spine of the book.

Rogoff and colleagues (Rogoff, Paradise, Arauz, Correa-Chavez, & Angelillo, 2003) call learning through such close watching and hearing "intent participation":

> Learning through keen observation and listening…seems to be especially valued and emphasized in communities where children have access to learning from informal community involvement. They observe and listen with intent concentration and initiative…their collaborative participation is expected when they are ready to help in shared endeavors. (p. 176)

Although she had books and other reading material in her home, Mrs. McPheeters did not have the opportunity to experience intent participation in a library. Until she was 5 years old, she lived on farms. One of them "tucked in the backwoods of Rome, Georgia, had about it a certain idyllic appearance with its fertile low lands, its wooded hillsides where grew wild flowers—violets, honeysuckle and a variety of others" (1988, p. 100). But the community had few educational resources, aside from the Baptist church, which had monthly services and school three or four times a year. She had a handful of books at home, including the Bible, Aesop's *Fables*, and the Sears & Roebuck catalogue, which "served me in several capacities, picture book, reader, speller and arithmetic" (p. 101). Annie McPheeters' interest in books was nurtured in the home, mainly by her mother, who had an eighth-grade education. McPheeters writes, "She was an avid reader and it is to her that I attribute a large part of my interest in books and reading" (p. 100). When the family moved to the city of Rome, McPheeters entered the first grade in a segregated school.

Zora Neale Hurston had books in her home. One day, two White women visited her school in Eatonville, and Hurston read so well that the women gave her three books before they left Florida and subsequently sent her a box of books. It contained, among others, *Gulliver's Travels* and a book of Greek and Roman myths. Hurston's mother introduced her to the Bible and monitored homework times with Hurston's seven siblings.

Randall Robinson's home was filled with books: "Mama and Daddy loved books. Books were all around us, hers mostly religious, his political. Everyone read, and talked incessantly about what they'd read" (1999, p. 21).

One international study (Evans, Kelley, Sikora, & Treiman, 2010) identified parental scholarly culture as a powerful resource that increases the amount of school that children complete. Parental scholarly culture is defined as an environment wherein books in the home are plentiful, used, and enjoyed; the educational advantages such culture confers can be found across rich and poor nations, economic systems, and historical periods. For African Americans in segregated communities, where public library service was absent or inadequate, a home rich in books or literacy activities (such as storytelling) gave necessary food for the soul and the intellect.

*   *   *

Together, the park, the school, the business district, the library, and people in the frame houses that lined the blocks in the neighborhood gave us some of the life that I could only glimpse in the pictures of little White children in the pages of *My Weekly Reader, Childcraft, The Friendly Village,* and all the other reading materials that we used. I imagined that life to be unfettered, with access to warmth and support, to the kind of full-out acceptance and positive feedback that we associate with unconditional love. I thought the White children in these books were beneficiaries of childhood experiences that would lead them to be anything they wanted to be. After the adults explained why I could only use the colored ladies restroom in the basements of department stores—even when I had to go urgently while four floors away—and why all the people in our neighborhood were Black, I learned that along with support, protection, discipline, and opportunity, the community folks were preparing my siblings, friends, and me to brace ourselves for the inevitable time when we had to leave our community for the world beyond. Many years later, reminded of the rich social spaces of my neighborhood, I studied children's interactions with "community coaches," caring people who imparted local knowledge and skills.[7]

We children learned from community coaches that benefits would be generous for those who met community expectations and who tempered the negative messages—from movies, books, political speeches, and face-to-face contact—that seeped through permeable neighborhood boundaries. Yet conflicting communications confused me, as they did others of my generation. In his autobiography, Randall Robinson (1998) writes, "Seen, known, appreciated, nurtured by ours, scarcely visible to theirs" (p. 20). Invisibility is a long-standing theme of how people construct notions of race using social, rather biological criteria. Two landscapes, one White and one Black, existed with separate political, residential, and educational spaces.

> Whether it was Jefferson's manipulation of the landscape and his program to conceal from view the black slaves working at Monticello, the separate "colored" entrance to the cinema, or simply the denial of access to certain facilities, the effect was to render the black person invisible. (Barton, 2001, p. 5)

Crossing the boundaries between those landscapes would be for some African American children the equivalent of an unforgettable coming of age, perhaps a traumatic rite of passage. I am sure that parents and other community adults faced this dilemma: How to prepare children for the inevitable confrontation with a society that devalued us, or to explain racism after a compelling personal incident. In *The Immortal Child*, Du Bois (1920) offered this advice:

> The truth lies ever between extremes. It is wrong to introduce the child to race consciousness prematurely; it is dangerous to let that consciousness grow spontaneously without intelligent guidance. With every step of dawning intelligence, explanation—frank, free, guiding explanation—must come. The day will dawn when mother must explain gently but clearly why the little girls next door do not want to play with "niggers"; what the real cause is of the teacher's unsympathetic attitude; and how people may ride in the backs of street cars and the smoker end of trains and still be people, honest high-minded souls. (p. 204)

Change

In 1959, when I was 12, my parents moved us away from Washington Park. We went to Clayton County, then a rural area contiguous to Fulton County, Georgia (Atlanta is the county seat). We became the first family to live in Paradise Park, a large tract of land sold in half-acre parcels to Black buyers. Our house was on a dirt road, and we had well water and a septic tank. Daddy, my uncle and Papa, friends, and contractors built our house, a large, three-bedroom brick rambler. My parents had wanted to establish their own household, and Daddy wanted a piece of land larger than the city parcels in West Atlanta, where the Black population was building the spacious homes that have made the city proud.

Ours was the first house; soon after, a few small, prefabricated wood-frame houses would be built. As a child, I mourned the loss of the old neighborhood. Playmates for my siblings and me were rarely around. I took long bicycle rides on the weekend, first for comfort and then simply for the sake of renewal and curiosity. One day I found a decaying wooden school-house next to a cemetery and a church; on another, I explored a creek free-ly until wildlife (like a rabbit, a snake, or stray dog) wandered in crackling underbrush of the banks and frightened me away. In *Belonging: A Culture of Place,* bell hooks, who returned as an adult to live in her native Kentucky, captures the way she learned to honor nature. She writes,

> Freely roaming Kentucky hills in childhood, running from snakes and all forbidden outside terrors both real and imaginary, I learned to be safe in the knowledge that facing what I fear and moving beyond it will keep me secure. With this knowledge I nurtured a sublime trust in the power of nature to seduce, excite, delight, and solace. (hooks, 2009, p. 6)

To this day, I have mixed feelings about the natural world. Someplace—perhaps in Washington Park in the little body that propelled me across the concrete sewerage pipe and up the ladder to which no slide was attached—a warning voice had emerged and whispered: danger sometimes lurks amid order and verdant beauty.

Starting in the fifth grade after we moved to Clayton County, I attended Cooper Street School, located in one of the most impoverished neighbor-hoods in Atlanta, for the last 2 years of elementary school. My mother taught kindergarten there, and the school authorities permitted my sister and me to attend. I visited with my best friend sometimes after school. We would walk to her house, a tiny, neat three-room cottage. On the way, we had passed, here and there, boarded up bungalows, their yards overgrown. Looking back, I recall no markers of a network of learning in the vicinity of the school. Al-though the school had a fair measure of protection in caring teachers and student activities (e.g., the safety patrol, as shown in Figure 2.6), there were no green spaces nearby, no recreation centers or stores (save for very small storefronts), and few churches.

Almost every day, the children of Cooper Street School and their fami-lies taught me something new about the meaning of poverty. Some students came in ragged clothes. Some, like my friend, lived with their families in houses that seemed built for one or two people at most. Other children were hungry. During the late 1950s, when I attended Cooper Street, the Na-tional School Lunch Program served only a small proportion of poor chil-dren (see Levine, 2008). Teachers often contributed money to buy lunches for students. Field trips were rare; we went to places that had no admission fees, yet welcomed Black children: the zoo; the county fair; the campuses of

Figure 2.6   Safety Patrol, Cooper Street School, Atlanta, 1957. *Source:* Personal collection of Saundra Rice Murray Nettles.

Atlanta's historically Black colleges and universities, which included Spelman, Morehouse, Clark, and Morris Brown Colleges; the Interdenominational Theological Center; and Atlanta University. The students at Cooper Street School received few gifts. I recall one day in fifth grade, I listed the toys I received at Christmas: a doll, plastic building blocks, a doctor's kit, shoes, and dresses. The child who spoke after me said an apple and a pair of socks. Other children each mentioned a single, precious gift: a toy gun, a pair of skates, a book. Looking down, I blushed with shame; I had so much and they had so little.

Also, I was the teacher's kid, and that set me apart. But my mother encouraged me to fend for myself rather than seeking refuge in her classroom when the inevitable conflicts among peers occurred. It was one of those conflicts that sent me to the principal's office, the only time in my school career. I had swung wildly at Elizabeth after she ripped my safety patrol badge from my favorite blouse. I had been on duty, assisting the crossing guard and standing with my arms outstretched in the middle of Cooper Street. The principal, Mr. Crawl, was appalled at our behavior, but he told us so in kind, direct terms, reminding us that we had violated the school's slogan, painted in blue letters over the arch of the main stairway: "Walk the

World with Dignity." As I recall, he suspended us from class the next day to make it very clear.

Elizabeth and I never became friends, but we never fought again, partly out of respect for Mr. Crawl, who had modeled that quality by treating us gently and in equal measure, but also, I think, by respect for each other.

*   *   *

Living away from Georgia during the 1960s and 1970s, I had heard rumblings about the state of my old neighborhood network in Atlanta. A single mother, whose extended family had lived next door ever since I could remember, was murdered at home. I heard rumors that one of her relatives might have committed the deed, but in those times, people closed ranks and kept quiet about the drearier aspects of community life. Folks whispered when they spoke of drugs entering the streets around Washington Park. Aging residents, who had meticulously tended their yards and houses, were less able to summon the energy to make repairs, sweep the cement driveways, and plant flowers. My aunt and uncle sent their children to a newly integrated school outside the neighborhood. Visiting my grandparents and other relatives who lived in the big old house on Desoto Street, I witnessed the early stages of decay in the physical and social fabric. The streets where I had played rock school and hopscotch were strangely quiet.

The internal wear and tear was nothing compared with what MARTA (the Metropolitan Atlanta Rapid Transit Authority) would do. Parts of the neighborhood became construction sites during the installation of rapid rail lines for one of the stations. The Washington Park swimming pool, a source of communal pride and pleasurable memories, was one of many casualties. According to a 1999 article,

> That history was disrupted in a pronounced way in the 1960s, when MARTA took apart the pool to make room for the proposed construction of the rapid rail's west line. The loss of the pool came on the heels of a community in flux anyway, since now residents and businesses could move to areas once prohibited to them by segregation. (Swimming Upstream, 1999)

Like urban renewal projects in other places, houses and other buildings were torn down. One of them was my music teacher's. The store was demolished. My aunt, a native of Washington, DC, who has lived in the neighborhood since 1957, summed up the human toll it took on one person, an Atlanta University professor who was forced to relocate due to the

MARTA project: "He died not long after he moved," she said. "You can't say it was the physical cause of death, but I know he didn't want to move, and he wasn't the same after he did" (Roots, 1999).

Paradise Park (the subdivision to which we had moved) was once verdant and sparsely developed. It became a dumping ground for trash, old cars, and other junk. A road adjacent to the property was widened and small businesses, including a crematorium and facility for medical and malodorous wastes, were opened. "Progress" was strangely linked to loss and disintegration. Changes came, not just in my small world of home, school, and our nascent recognition of class differences within the African American community, but in the very geography of where Black people could live, work, and learn. External forces—such as disinvestment in inner city neighborhoods, desegregation and its consequences—put in motion these changes in my neighborhood and other Black communities across the country. In *The Truly Disadvantaged*, William J. Wilson (1987) argued that, beginning in the 1970s, Black employment decreased in inner cities due to structural changes in the economy (e.g., shift from manufacturing to services) and, at the same time, working-class and middle-class Blacks moved to higher-income neighborhoods in the city and the suburbs. The result was concentrated neighborhood poverty, which is measured by characteristics such as the percentage of individuals below poverty, percentage of unemployed, percentage of households headed by women and have children, and percentage of families receiving public assistance. According to a report on the 2000 Census from the Annie E. Casey Foundation (Mather & Rivers, 2006), some 44.7% of impoverished Black children lived in "severely distressed neighborhoods," defined as neighborhoods with high drop-out rates, high male unemployment, high percentages of families headed by single parents, and high poverty rates. The vast majority of these neighborhoods were in metropolitan areas; the top 4 of 10 were in the South.

Conditions in highly impoverished neighborhoods are associated with behavioral, health, and academic problems. As David Berliner (2005) pointed out in his presidential address at the American Educational Research Association, "Although the power of schools and educators to influence individual students is never to be underestimated, the out-of-school factors associated with poverty play both a powerful and a limiting role in what can actually be achieved" (p. 2). To improve outcomes for children through the design of neighborhood interventions, researchers are beginning to examine how places make a difference in children's everyday lives (see, for example, Kawachi & Berkman, 2003 on health and Nettles, Caughy, & O'Campo, 2008 on school adjustment in the early grades). One recent finding of note (Caughy, Nettles, & Lima, 2011) is that in neighborhoods where adults were willing to assist children in need and to intervene in acts of delinquency and child misbehavior, Black parents were much more likely to give messages to first graders about racial pride combined with messages about how to cope with discrimination. Such combined messages were also associated with fewer behavior problems.

This is a promising sign that vibrant networks of learning still exist and continue to prepare children to resist oppression and discrimination. Stephen Berrey (2009), who examined oral histories of Black rural Mississippians born and reared in the 1930s through 1950s, tells us,

> As interviewees discuss their childhood—who nurtured them, who taught them life lessons, who taught them how to act in Jim Crow society—they describe a network of individuals in the community, including both men and women.... Grandparents, aunts and uncles, and neighbors were members of a family unit that helped children learn racial rules and unlearn ideologies of black inferiority. (p. 67)

Teachers and other adults told stories about Black pain and struggle as part of this curriculum of place and modeled appropriate behavior. Moreover, interviewees described "a major characteristic of racial lessons: varying one's response based on particular contexts" (p. 82). Children learned flexibility—when to avoid confrontation, when to speak up, when to take concerted action—from the community as home.

Envision one Black child, Anne McPheeters. She is in the third or fourth grade and has exhausted her supply of reading materials at home and at school. She decides to go to her town's Carnegie Library, a place that none of the Black people she knows has ever entered. Climbing the two flights of stairs to the front door, she sees the librarian, a White woman, sitting at the desk. The librarian stands up, comes toward the child, and says, "Go back, you cannot come in here." McPheeters writes, "Stunned, I stood still. Finally as I turned to go and with tears in my eyes and a heart full of hurt, I turned to her and said, 'I'm leaving now, but I promise that one of these days I'll be back and won't have to leave'" (p. 102).

Notes

1. Edna Louise Lewis Rice, interview by Saundra Rice Murray Nettles, May 21, 2005, Morrow, Georgia, field notes.
2. In 2006, the U.S. Congress designated the Gullah/Geechee Heritage Corridor, which includes the coastal counties of North Carolina, South Carolina, Georgia, and Florida, as one of 40 National Heritage Areas. These areas are defined as "places where natural, cultural, historic, and scenic resources com-

bine to form a cohesive, nationally important landscape arising from patterns of human activity shaped by geography" (National Park Service, 2012).

3. My mother refers to the American Beach on Amelia Island. American Beach lies about 5 miles from the city of Fernandina Beach, Florida (www.exploreAmelia.com). Abraham Lincoln Lewis, the first Black millionaire in Florida, bought parcels of land in 1935 to develop a resort for employees of the Pension Bureau of the Afro-American Life Insurance Company. In 2002, the resort town became the American Beach National Historic District (www.nationalreaisterefhistoricplaces.com/fl/Nassau/State.html). American Beach was one of many recreational resorts that African Americans established as alternatives to segregated facilities. See also Russ Rymer (1998), *American Beach: How "Progress" Robbed a Black Town—and Nation—of History, Wealth, and Power,*.

4. For a brief history of Blacks in the Boy Scouts, see "African Americans in the Boy Scout Movement." Retrieved from http://www.aaregistry.org/historic_events/view/african-americans-boy-scout-movement

5. Many children, especially those in urban areas, walk to school, although studies show that children are less likely to walk or bike when their parents are concerned with such factors as crime, after-school schedules, and traffic. In low-income neighborhoods, children who walk or bike to school do so regardless of whether the neighborhood is walkable or not (see Kerr, Rosenberg, Sallis, Frank, & Conway, 2006).

6. On her philosophy of working with children, McPheeters quotes Effie Power (1943), who wrote of pioneering librarians, "They saw in books and reading a way of life open to children and developed practical means of bringing children and books together." Power believed that the child needed to be guided in reading, guidance that extended beyond the classroom. The child "needed broad environments with which to grow physically, mentally and spiritually. Books and reading were influences which might supplement those of home and school in exceeding that environment" (Power, quoted in McPheeters, 1988, p. 29).

7. I have considered the practices of informal educators in everyday life within neighborhoods and community settings (McPartland & Nettles, 1991; Nettles, 1992). Some informal educators provide instruction on academic subjects, say reading, which have been previously introduced to the student by someone else. We call that "tutoring." Mentoring is another type of informal instruction involving an expert paired with a novice in supportive interactions for the learning of a skill, often practical (e.g.,workplace behavior) in nature.

"Coaching" is distinct from mentoring and tutoring. The term is used in diverse areas of performance, including sports, forensics, management, life skills, music and the arts, and in-service professional development of teachers. Coaching in community settings is described by examining research in three areas: (a) instruction as assisted performance (such as that which athletic coaches use); (b) the development of talent (in the arts and in sport); and (c) learning situated in authentic contexts, involving social interaction and collaboration. I observed community coaches in action: a policewoman supervising activities in a recreation center, two urban planners leading a class of third graders engaged in a city building activity, college students working with high school students in a leadership camp. My observations and review (1992) of related research revealed that the actions comprising coaching in community settings included all forms of teaching (e.g., telling, demonstrating); assessing the learner's performance; creating, selecting, or preparing the environment to create an optimal setting for learning; and providing social support (e.g., counseling, listening, protecting, advising, sharing, creating trust, and empathizing). Of all the instructional activities, providing time and space for practice was foremost.

3

Landscapes of Resistance

In "The Immortal Child," an essay on education and Black child development, W. E. B. Du Bois (1920) envisioned that the struggle to secure human rights and access to resources would not end in his time. Fighting for the goals of literacy, equal rights, and freedom from disease and economic want among Black children and their families and communities, Du Bois and his contemporaries continued the Black freedom struggle which, by the 20th century, had resulted in Black educational institutions, including colleges, industrial schools, and normal schools; Black self-help associations, whose outreach included health, education, and welfare; Black businesses; Black churches that served diverse needs of their congregations and nearby neighborhoods; spaces for learning in homes, school buildings, libraries, community centers; and restorative places such as natural landscapes and playgrounds.

Du Bois, widely regarded as the leading political and intellectual force in the modern American African freedom struggle, was one of the founders (along with John Dewey and others) of the National Association for the Advancement of Colored People (NAACP) in 1909. In 1910, Du Bois founded

Necessary Spaces, pages 55–86

and edited the organization's journal, *The Crisis*. His preoccupation with children's intellectual and racial development was already evident in his pioneering sociological work, *The Philadelphia Negro: A Social Study* (1899). He wrote,

> It is right and proper that Negro boys and girls should desire to rise as high in the world as their ability and just desert entitle them. They should be ever encouraged and urged to do so, although they should be taught also that idleness and crime are beneath and not above the lowest work. (pp. 390–391)

His concern for children was also expressed in the annual children's issue of *The Crisis*, and, in the 2 years it was published (1920 and 1921), in *The Brownies' Book: A Monthly Magazine for the Children of the Sun*, which Du Bois co-edited with poet, novelist, and essayist Jessie Fauset. The magazine was an explicit attempt to counteract the negative stereotyping of Black boys and girls (Lewis, 2000). The magazine featured photographs and illustrations of children of all ages, economic classes, and physical characteristics as well as poetry, short stories, games, information about Black achievers and leaders, and feedback to and from readers.[1]

To address health, educational and other needs, African American citizens of Du Bois' generation organized numerous community involvement programs and activities for children.

In 1908, Lugenia Burns Hope initiated the Atlanta Neighborhood Union (ANU) with eight middle-class women to address the need for services in Atlanta's poorest neighborhoods. Historian Cynthia Neverdon-Morton writes that the ANU enlisted Black women to meet two goals for education: first, "to provide playgrounds, clubs, good literature, and neighborhood centers for the moral, physical and intellectual development of the young" and second, "to establish lecture courses, classes, and clubs for the purpose of encouraging habits of cleanliness and industry, promoting child welfare, and bringing about culture and efficiency in general homemaking" (Neverdon-Morton, 1997, p. 45). When the organization disbanded in the 1970s, the ANU had implemented an impressive agenda, including community needs assessment, classes on personal and home care, after-school activities, several petitions for city services, and a settlement house (Rouse, 1995).

Prior to the 1919 Chicago Race Riot, Black churches there created the Sunday School League to play baseball in Chicago's Washington Park; the Cook County Baseball League excluded African Americans. Other groups concerned with children's health, such as the Urban League, settlement houses, and women's clubs, organized outdoor activities and pushed for access to nature as a source of renewal and escape from the dirt and congestion of the city (Fisher, 2006).

Black women in Harlem established the Utopia Children's House (UCH) in 1921 for disadvantaged children. The services included a preschool, an after-school program for older children, and for families, health care and recreation (Greenberg, 1991). In 1930, thirteen-year-old Jacob Lawrence (1917–2000) enrolled in the UCH arts and crafts program that James Wells, a member of Howard's faculty, had established, using the latest pedagogical theories that he had learned at Teachers College (Turner, 2000). Lawrence, who would later paint *The Life of Harriet Tubman* and *The Life of Frederick Douglass*, recalled trying different activities, including painting, woodwork, and soap carving. The UCH afforded him the experience of design, an awareness of, in Lawrence's words, "the world conceived and grasped as picture" (Turner, 2000, p. 99).

Growing up during the Great Depression, others of Lawrence's generation benefited from and added to the building of institutions in the Black community. As a child in Atlanta, I witnessed the flowering of local efforts. A fellow teacher with my father at Booker T. Washington High School from 1953 until 1968, J. W. Robinson, worked under a licensed architect for years designing homes for Atlanta's African American population (Lyon, 2009). After he obtained his license in 1970, he established his own firm; my uncle worked under him. My mother served a term as the president of the Bennett College alumni association; she and her two sisters had attended the college during the Depression. (During the economic downturn, their father had a steady job as a railway postal clerk.) The alumni club participated in various events, such as fashion shows to fund scholarships for deserving young women, and the annual Bennett-Morehouse choir concert.

But in Du Bois's view, "If the great battle of human right against poverty, against disease, against color prejudice is to be won, it must be won, not in our day, but in the day of our children's children" (Du Bois, 1920, p. 202). Du Bois' vision about the length of the battle was prescient. The Jim Crow era lasted well into the 1960s and affected the idealism of my generation, the so-called Baby Boomers. Following African Americans born during World War II, we boomers would continue to fight oppression as had generations before us, hoping to make big inroads into the seemingly intractable challenges of poverty, poor health, and racial discrimination.

*   *   *

When I was a little girl, it seemed that I spent all the Sundays of my childhood in church, Atlanta's Friendship Baptist, which my parents and my father's parents had attended since the 1920s. I lived for the day when

I could have communion like the grownups and older children. At age 7, when Rev. Samuel Williams baptized me, immersed me in the font at the left side of the pulpit, I finally experienced the beauty and anticipation of the words,

> Let us break bread together on our knees
> Let us break bread together on our knees
> When I fall on my knees with my face to the rising sun
> Oh Lord, have mercy on me.

Then the congregation ate the bread and it was hard, sticking in my throat until I washed it down with the grape juice that stood in for wine.

Rev. Williams preached the sermon, and in time, I came to appreciate the beauty and wisdom of his words. I hear him even now, in the voice and cadence of the scholar—he was chair of the religion and philosophy department at Morehouse—quoting the Scriptures and great intellects. He was also mentor for the Rev. Dr. Martin Luther King.

Rev. Williams seemed to be in dialogue with each person in the congregation, perhaps because he spoke from outlines, improvising between the phrases, such as "there is no one of us who has nothing to give," followed by Alfred Adler's theory of compensation, in a phrase, "there is no one of us who is so self-sufficient that he does not stand in the relation of receiver."[2]

Williams asked questions that engaged us, opening one sermon, for example, with "What is it that makes one truly great?" I can see him now, looking at us and pausing, inviting us to reflect and answer the question in our own minds. Rev. Williams continued, on this occasion, suggesting power and position as two attributes. But, he explained, these tend to corrupt because "man does not yet seem to know how to handle them." Rev. Williams said that there was but one way—"devotion to the service of others"—to resolve the inevitable conflict that aspiring to power and position produce. "True greatness lies in service to others,"[3] he concluded.

Reverend Sam, as some called him, was a tall man, bespectacled and of measured words. Most importantly, he modeled what he preached, notably in teaching and civil rights. As head of Atlanta's NAACP, he filed a federal suit in 1957 to desegregate the city's buses and trolleys. In 1960, he was a community leader and, along with Howard Zinn and Whitney Young, advised students who participated in direct action tactics (Atlanta Regional Council for Higher Education, 2005).

In 1957, I was 10 and learned about the Civil Rights Movement in church and at a distance—on the televised news, on the radio, and in the

Atlanta Constitution. In the continuing African American freedom struggle, children and youth would integrate schools, march in the streets, become martyrs. In 1955, for example, an African American boy named Emmet Till was beaten, shot, and thrown into a Mississippi river; he was only 14 years old.

In 1960, Ruby Bridges became the first African American child to attend an all-White public elementary school in the South; she was 6 years old when she attended the William Franz Elementary School in New Orleans (King, 2005). Norman Rockwell commemorated her first day in a painting, *The Problem We Live With,* which depicted the little girl in a white dress and pigtails walking with two White marshals in front and two White marshals behind her. The wall in the background shows "nigger" scrawled in large letters.

Across the South, parents and community members had prepared children to resist oppression. In his exploration of how African American children learned about race in rural Mississippi during the Jim Crow era, Stephen Berrey (2009) tells us that "a closer examination of the black family reveals that, within the everyday realm, African Americans—as mothers, as fathers, as relatives, as neighbors—were participating in a larger daily struggle and were contributing to what would eventually become a mass movement" (pp. 68–69). Wilma King (1995) comments that even while enslaved, "the age at which youngsters actively opposed slavery is significant since children had to be mature enough to understand their condition and the potential for change" (p. 116). Acts of resistance included running away and pretending to be ill, but becoming literate was the ultimate act during slavery and after. As Heather Andrea Williams writes in *Self Taught: African American Education in Slavery and Freedom,* "Understanding how enslaved people learned not only illuminates the importance of literacy as an instrument of resistance and liberation, but also brings into view the clandestine tactics and strategies that enslaved people employed to gain some control over their own lives" (Williams, 2005, pp. 7–8).

Charlayne Hunter-Gault, who, with Hamilton Holmes, would be the first Black students to integrate the University of Georgia in 1961, wrote about the Atlanta Student Movement in her memoir, *In My Place* (1992). She said that change was evident in Atlanta and in the students in the movement: "We had been protected and privileged within the confines of our segregated communities. But now that we students had removed the protective covering, we could see in a new light both our past and our future" (p. 144). She identifies slavery and segregation as "a system designed to keep us in our place and convince us, somehow, that it was our fault, as well as our destiny. Now, without either ambivalence or shame, we saw ourselves as heirs to a legacy of struggle" (p. 144).

Hunter-Gault's friend, Carolyn Long, was one of 4,000 university students in Atlanta's Student Movement. According to Long (quoted in Hunter-Gault's memoir), the city's movement excluded high school students: "One of the things we decided was that we wouldn't have any high-school student demonstrators, because we didn't think they could take the pressure and the harassment that we anticipated from the white waitresses, the white customers, and the white police " (p. 140). But some of us attempted to resist in other, less visible ways.

*   *   *

In fall of 1961, my family had been living in rural Clayton County for nearly 3 years. This trip would be a break in our usual weekend chores; Daddy and I were on the way to the home of the Massachusetts Institute of Technology (MIT) alumnus who would be interviewing me as part of the admissions process. I had come to the attention of an Institute recruiter because I had built a solar house, entered it in the citywide science fair, and won a gold medal and a citation in the Future Scientists of America award program, sponsored by Ford Motor Company.

The house was a scale model, painted black (Figure 3.1). On its roof was the solar cell that I had ordered from a company that advertised in *Mechanix Illustrated.* My father had helped me hook the cell to a tiny flashlight bulb, which glowed for one moment when I flicked a switch. Every day for 8 or 9 months before the science fair, I had stayed up late at night to read about the sun, design the house, and with my father, cut and nail rectangular pieces of wood for the model.

Now, we pulled into a driveway. The house was a single-story, a rambler like ours. But the length, the fine details of the trim, and the location set this one apart. I stepped from the car, grinned at my father, took a deep breath. Time to go on stage. I quickly ran through all the admonitions passed down from my mother and teachers: Don't chew gum. Don't sit with your legs open. Say "sir." Look interested. Speak softly and distinctly. Smile.

He answered the door bell, glanced at his watch.

"I expected you people at four."

"I'm sorry, sir," my father said. "We've never been to this neighborhood before and it took us a little while to find your house."

We went inside. Our host directed us to a sofa. Holding the application in his hand, the alumnus sat in a chair across the room. He frowned and looked at my father.

Figure 3.1   Saundra Rice explaining the Solar House, 1961.

"Well, George. I see here that your little girl wants to go up north to the Institute." He paused, "I went to MIT. My son is there now." His soft drawl still lingering in the air, he glanced in my direction. "He's studying to be an architectural engineer. One day he might take over my firm."

I smiled, thinking this was my cue to state my aspirations. But the alumnus continued, holding my gaze in his. "There's something you should know," he said. "We don't want any women at the Institute. We don't want any nigras at the Institute. We especially don't want any nigra women at the Institute."

Finally, he smiled. Then he looked at my father, who did exactly what I knew he would do. He probably saw no other way. Teachers in the Atlanta Public Schools had been warned that they would lose their jobs if they participated in antisegregation efforts.

He stood up, motioned "stand up, honey" to me and smiled at that man.

"Thank you so much, sir. Saundra and I appreciate your time. We'll be going now."

He walked us to the door. I heard him murmur, "Try Spelman College. Fine college for nigra girls."

We drove off. We had no trouble finding our way out of the neighborhood. Soon we were on the highway toward home.

"It's alright, honey. Maybe the recruiter can find someone else to interview you. The one back there was just a little prejudiced."

"I know, Daddy. I'm OK."

My father said nothing more. He concentrated on the driving.

I was 14, a child just out of thick braids and dresses with wide lace collars and satin sashes. I looked down at my hands and, to keep my father from worrying, glanced up occasionally to look out of the window. When we arrived home, he told my mother what had happened; thereafter, we seldom mentioned it.

Looking back, I think I have finally figured out why my father remained silent. He had moved his family from the city to what I considered a backwater so that we could have a chance to have an unfettered childhood. Before we left Washington Park, shocking events had entered our lives. I have a vivid, accurate memory of one incident.

Two of our cousins lived on one of the streets near the elementary school in the neighborhood. When my siblings and I visited them, we often played games outside. Sometimes Bobby, the older boy who lived next door, joined us. He was in the eighth grade at Washington High School, where my father taught mathematics. One day, Bobby was stabbed by another boy while serving detention; the shop teacher had kept them after school because they were fighting in class. Our playmate stumbled upstairs to the principal's office; my father happened to be there. Bobby died in my father's arms. At home, when I overheard the adults talking about what had happened, I became frightened. I thought about the awful event and asked, Why?

After that, my father seemed to intensify his efforts to move us to the country. My parents were able to afford lots in the undeveloped county; Daddy and his friends built the house, a rambler (now known as "midcentury modern") in a setting that came to resemble an African compound combined with the American dream: two wooden outbuildings, a gazebo, a pool, a large vegetable garden in the back, a swing for children, and my mother's flowers in the front yard. Foremost, Daddy had returned to the home ground of his childhood. Our house was about 10 minutes away from Ellenwood, Georgia, where his father's boyhood farm had been located, and 20 minutes from McDonough, his mother's home.

Perhaps that day in the car while we drove home, my father realized that moving had not insulated us from the ugliness of racial segregation. Somewhere deep inside, I asked the same question I had of Bobby's death: Why?

A Convergence of Social Forces

I found solace at Sunday dinner in my grandparents' home and at church, listening closely to Rev. Williams when he preached at Friendship. Rev. Williams had an abiding concern for young people. From the pulpit, he spoke many times about family and home as the place for "rectification," the place for providing the right environment:

> I define environment as the system of relations in which an organism may find what is needed for its growth and development or in which it may find a system of relations which will do just the opposite, i.e., militate against growth and development. Parents must decide which of these their home is going to be.

His notes show that he examined this theme in several ways, for example "outlook on life = attributes towards others—race relations for example!" and "security and confidence for the child."[4]

Once he said the only words that I recall clearly. "Saundra, you are a bright young woman, but you won't ever have the luxury of just being an intellectual." I know now what he meant, but at the time, it was just another wise thing that he said as he attended our plays and picnics and visited in our homes.

Meanwhile, African American children were activists and martyrs in the freedom struggle. On May 2 and 3, 1963, several hundred Black boys and girls marched in the Birmingham Children's Crusade. Taylor Branch (1988) gives this account:

> Reporters saw things they had never seen before. George Wall, a tough-looking police captain, confronted a group of thirty-eight elementary-school children and did his best to cajole or intimidate them into leaving the lines, but they all said they knew what they were doing. Asked her age as she climbed into a paddy wagon, a tiny girl called out that she was six. (p. 757)

My family, indeed the world, saw television images of police violence against children; they were hosed, clubbed, and attacked by dogs. Police arrested and jailed many of the marchers.

On September 22, 1963, four Black girls were killed when the Ku Klux Klan bombed the 16th Street Baptist Church in Birmingham. Addie Mae Collins, Carole Robertson, and Cynthia Wesley were 14 years old. Denise McNair was only 11.

That fall, I was beginning freshman year at Bennett College, which my mother and her two sisters attended in the 1930s. Like Atlanta's Spelman College, Bennett offered an excellent liberal arts education for African American women. Still feeling sadness, fear, and anger about the murders of four innocent children, I was en route to my German class on November 22, 1963, when I learned that President Kennedy had been assassinated. Amid the shock and sadness that gripped the nation, I and other Bennett students wondered what would happen to Kennedy's civil rights agenda and his "New Frontier," legislation that established programs such as ones to stem unemployment and establish community mental health centers. After taking office, President Johnson continued and expanded the New Frontier, which became "The Great Society," a set of domestic programs whose major goals included the elimination of racial injustice and poverty.

Along with a great many other young people, I had high hopes that the Civil Rights Act of 1964 and the War on Poverty, which President Johnson also launched in 1964, would provide effective weapons in the struggle against poverty. I imagined that "maximum feasible participation," which the Economic Opportunity Act of 1964 called for, would energize local participation. Citizens would take an active part in the planning and implementing of War on Poverty programs and services. Surely, maximum feasible participation would tap into historical traditions of self-help and grassroots social activism in Black communities.

* * *

I came of age working in Great Society programs. Inspired by my pastor in Atlanta, I majored in philosophy at predominately Black Howard University, to which I had transferred after my freshman year; and at the end of my sophomore year, was one of thousands of volunteers who worked with preschool children in the summer of 1965 when the Head Start program, one of the first interventions in the War on Poverty, was launched.

The program would be built on an emerging body of evidence, which suggested that the cycle of poverty could be interrupted through early childhood education. As the *Recommendations for a Head Start Program* stated,

There is considerable evidence that the early years of childhood are the most critical point in the poverty cycle. During these years the creation of learning patterns, emotional development and the formation of individual expectations and aspirations take place at a very rapid pace. For the child of poverty there are clearly observable deficiencies in the processes which lay the foundation for a pattern of failure—and thus a pattern of poverty—throughout the child's entire life. (Head Start, 1972, p. 2)

Head Start was designed to be comprehensive, with health services, social services, cognitive development programs, and parent participation programs.

I recall little from that summer in Head Start, save for my intense exhaustion. I was grateful for naptime after running after 4-year old children on the playground, comforting them during physical examinations, eating breakfast and lunch and chatting about the events in their days, wiping noses, assisting the teachers with circle time and learning activities, and above all, being responsible for multiple, fragile lives.

During my junior year, one of my professors who taught political philosophy told me to apply for a job in a new antipoverty program, Upward Bound. Supporting young African Americans' efforts to attend college, he reasoned, would prepare me for a life of service. During the academic year, on weekends, high school students would be enrolled in special courses to improve their writing and math skills, and the "program assistants," as we college students were called, would engage them in enriching activities—debates and conversations about issues of the day, museum visits, concerts, and the like.

The Upward Bound students benefited from the atmosphere of the Howard campus in the 1960s, where great scholars, such as Drs. Frank M. Snowden and Eleanor W. Traylor, taught undergraduate and graduate students alike. During academic year 1966–1967, the centennial of Howard's founding, the Upward Bound students discussed the lives and contributions of key leaders who lectured on campus that year: Martin Luther King, Adam Clayton Powell Jr., and President Johnson. The students also glimpsed the beginnings of the campus protests that became part of converging, multiple social movements in the 1960s: the Civil Rights Movement, the feminist movement, the antiwar movement, the technological revolution, and the Black Power movement. None of us—program assistants and high school participants alike—had any inkling that programs like Head Start and Upward Bound represented the beginnings of large-scale formal programming for low income children and youth.

After graduating in 1967 from Howard, I attended the University of Illinois Graduate School of Library and Information Science. Although the graduate school had one of the best programs in the country, I missed my work with kids in the Upward Bound program, and the other opportunities that Howard had afforded: seeing African Americans every day in roles as diverse as professors and deans to students in every major and cafeteria workers and hospital orderlies; hanging out with friends over meals and in the dorms; weekend parties; and the cultural life of Washington. At Illinois, Black students from all over the world were only about 1% of the 30,000 student population, and I never met any Black professors. Walking along the main streets in Urbana that made that place a college town, I longed for the jumble of small coffee houses, beauty shops, storefront churches, and chicken joints along Georgia Avenue, the street that ran from the suburbs of Silver Spring, Maryland, to its ending as Seventh Street near the waterfront in southwest DC.

In my last semester at Illinois, just before spring break in 1968, Martin Luther King was killed. I watched the fires that burned on the South Side as my plane descended into Chicago, a stopover en route to Atlanta. That same spring, on the eve of a job interview at the Library of Congress, I wondered about the fate of the Great Society programs as I watched television from my hotel across from the White House. Lyndon Johnson, champion of these programs, announced that he would not seek a second term as president. The Vietnam War weighed heavily in his thinking, but the programs continued and, when I returned to Washington for the job at the Library of Congress, I resumed service in them—first as a volunteer at Legal Aid in an H Street office and subsequently as a volunteer for Friendship House, a private agency in the settlement house tradition and recipient of a small amount of federal funds. I loved to visit the old building, a Capitol Hill mansion in which Francis Scott Key, who wrote the Star Spangled Banner, once lived. Working at Friendship House was the start of many years that I spent in the southeast quadrant of the city.

Rev. Williams died unexpectedly in 1970. By then he had co-founded the Southern Christian Leadership Conference (SCLC), chaired the Atlanta Community Relations Commission, presided over the Atlanta Branch of the NAACP, and led civil rights protests. He led our church in building housing for low-income residents.

He was my first mentor. Rev. Williams inspired my commitment to social justice and to working with neighborhood adults and youth who wanted to invest time, energy, and other resources in the education, health, and economic well-being of community residents. I think of him often, still saddened by the loss of his wisdom, his intellect, his passionate desire for human rights.

As a young adult in the 1970s and 1980s, I witnessed the deterioration in the cities that I frequented most often: Washington, DC; Baltimore; Chicago; and Atlanta. Studying for a doctorate in psychology at Howard as a mentee of feminist psychologist Dr. Martha T. Mednick, I noticed the changes in the blocks adjacent to the university's campus and in the Washington neighborhoods where my husband and I lived. The merchants gradually closed themselves off from clients with shutters, bars, and bulletproof plastic. Riding the bus south on Georgia Avenue, I saw boarded-up houses and the swings and other playground equipment in disrepair at the Robert Kennedy playground. One of the elderly librarians at the university moved from her house (a block from campus) because she feared for her safety. Libraries shortened their hours due to a decline in users.

As neighborhood conditions worsened, practitioners and academics honed and offered their skills to design, implement, and assess the effectiveness of systems that increasingly supplemented or even supplanted local, "natural" ways of socializing and educating children and youth for an increasingly complex world. Early on, local governments limited citizen input, seeing "maximum feasible participation" as a threat to entrenched power (Bae, 2011). Policymakers, academics, and scholar-activists like me would fill some of the gaps—collecting data on community needs, positing theoretical rationales, designing programs, and evaluating program impacts. I was aware of and sometimes participated in new professions and subdivisions that were added within existing scholarly disciplines: among them, youth development, applied developmental psychology, and social entrepreneurship. But would our efforts to end poverty and assure positive development of marginalized children displace grassroots involvement, or repair and enrich networks of learning that had contributed to the social and academic development of Black children over generations? Perhaps, more importantly, would formal programs provide the contexts for children to develop competencies needed to resist the status quo that continues to impoverish and deny opportunities to the great share of Black children?

Everyday Resistance in the Family and Community

Despite the changes in existing networks of learning and the emergence of formal, government and philanthropic educational and social programs, Black parents and community members continued to exert their influence to assure adequate, even excellent, preparation. Sometimes, that took the form of active management of where children were educated. Economically stable Black families who lived in urban neighborhoods might send their children to schools beyond the geographic boundaries of their communities. For example, Lorene Cary, who in 1972 would enter traditionally male and White St. Paul's School in New Hampshire, attended Lea School, a public elementary school near the University of Pennsylvania, not in her West Philly school district. Just as Charlayne Hunter-Gault joined the Atlanta Student Movement, saying, "We were simply doing what we were born and raised to do" (Hunter-Gault, 1992, p. 144), Cary writes that she felt compelled to go to St. Paul's because her upbringing had prepared her for it. Why, Cary asks in her 1991 memoir, *Black Ice*, had her mother

> dragged me across the street on my knees when I balked on the morning before the big I.Q. test, the one that could get me into the top first-grade class, the class on which free instrument and French lessons, advanced Saturday-morning classes, and a special, individualized reading series were bestowed? (p. 32)

As other young people who had participated among the leading edge to integrate schools and other public places, Cary had a sense that she was obligated to join the effort. She writes, "Wasn't it time for me to play my part in that mammoth enterprise—the integration, the moral transformation, no less, of America?" (pp. 32–33).

In impoverished urban communities, there were hopeful signs of parental and community involvement in educational matters. In the media, grassroots projects surfaced—ones that would motivate other efforts and be sustainable with volunteer, modest funding, and other resources from the community. In 1974, Washington, DC, single parent Kimi Gray started a college fund called "College Here We Come" (Simons, 1978). She collected dues of 50¢ a week from fellow residents in the Kenilworth-Parkside, a sprawling public housing complex; met weekly with students; and with assistance from a local community-based agency, matched students with tutors, jobs, and help with applications for college admission and scholarships. A tall and heavyset woman when I met her in the 1980s, Gray had five children by the time she was 19 years old, and she had lived in public housing for most of her life. She was determined that her children and others in Kenilworth-Parkside would become self-sufficient despite the often deplorable conditions at the housing complex: drug dealing, rat infestation, barren yards, and leaking roofs. She and other parents encouraged students to open bank accounts and save their earnings for college. By 1989, some 600 students had gone to college. Prior to the founding of the program, Gray reported, only two students from the housing complex had attended college (Osborne, 1989).[5] In another example, Push for Excellence, a grassroots effort that Rev. Jesse Jackson started in 1975, quickly grew from concerted local actions to a national movement (Murray Nettles et al., 1982).

* * *

In 1984, anticipating yet another divide between rich and poor, Dr. Jesse Bemley came to my office at the United Planning Organization (UPO), a large antipoverty agency in Washington, DC, to discuss ways to put computers in poor communities. Bemley, a father and full-time information technology professional, founded Joint Educational Facilities (JEF) to promote free courses in computer literacy for children in some of the city's poorest neighborhoods. He had purchased computer equipment and taught courses after work hours, believing that without extensive grassroots initiatives, the number of African American students receiving degrees in science and engineering would not change from existing levels. One of five children reared by a mother who left the welfare rolls to become a domestic, Dr. Bemley had majored in mathematics and also had taken education courses (J. Bemley, personal communication, April 1, 2004).

As director of the Office of Field Services Operations with responsibility for community-based neighborhood centers scattered throughout the city and a former information systems analyst, I was the most likely person in the organization to suggest a place to start in avoiding a potential opportunity gap, which soon came to be called, the "Digital Divide." But in 1984, when Dr. Bemley and I met, the gap had received only passing mention, for example, in Senator Frank Lautenberg's 1983 speech to the U.S. Senate (Compaine, 2001) and in a study conducted by Johns Hopkins Center for Social Organization of Schools (Becker, 1982).

We tried but failed to place free computers in an elementary school and created a plan for the "Neighborhood Computer Club," which would meet in recreation centers and apartment buildings. Literacy was the main goal, but Dr. Bemley wanted club members to go beyond the basics to an understanding of the design principles of computer languages. Although many people enthusiastically reviewed the plan for a citywide network of computer clubs, the project was not funded. Antipoverty funds for basic needs—food, shelter, fuel—had been curtailed, and agencies like ours were trying to identify ways to become less dependent on federal and local funding. Dr. Bemley continued with JEF, building it as an all-volunteer, community-based organization. In addition to local organizing, in the 1980s he began efforts to encourage the participation of Black high school and college students in engineering and computing professional activities, such as national and international conferences and symposia. He organized the High School Computer Competition at the national conference of the Black Data Processing Associates (BDPA); winning competitors are eligible to compete for the Dr. Jesse Bemley Scholarship (BDPA Black Education and Technology Foundation, 2011).

* * *

I started conducting educational research at Hopkins in the mid-1980s, around the time that Ta-Nehisi Coates was a Black boy becoming a man in inner-city Baltimore. In his 2009 memoir, *The Beautiful Struggle*, he writes about his life at home, at school, and in the city streets, particularly in Mondawmin, the West Baltimore neighborhood in which he grew up. Parents became more vigilant, especially when vicious whips of heroin and crack sales and addiction hit neighborhoods.

I recognized Coates's parents in my Baltimore family. Ever since my twin daughters were born in 1976, I had called Maryland my second home. My children were born in Columbia, Maryland, one of the first new towns in the U.S. suburbs. The children's grandparents, Donald Sr. and Rosa Murray, lived in West Baltimore; we spent nearly every Sunday there beginning in the 1970s, when I taught at the University of Maryland Baltimore County. The Murrays talked about race, read about the glories and problems of Black folk in library books and books they bought, monitored the behavior of their three sons, and supported the NAACP and other causes. Coates's parents were "Conscious," a word he uses to describe the Black person's critical awareness of the collective plight of Black people in the world, the continuing commitment to deep understanding of the historic forces contributing to that condition, and engagement in the struggle and resistance against those forces. The Coates's home overflowed with books, a great many about African and African American history. (Coates's father, W. Paul Coates, is founding publisher of Black Classic Press). In elementary school, Coates participated in his father's "compulsory book-of-the-month club selected from what we considered obscure and irrelevant" (Coates, 2009, p. 24), but Ta-Nehisi did poorly in learning what he called the Great Knowledge, "taught from our lives' beginnings, whether we realized it or not. Street professors presided over invisible corner podiums, and the Knowledge was dispensed. . . . They lectured from sacred texts like Basic Game, Applied Cool, Barbershop 101" (Coates, 2009, p. 36). When he entered William H. Lemmel Junior High School, he says, "I was a monument to unknowledge" (p. 36). He was not street-smart, not wise in the ways of urban life described in books that scholars published in the latter years of the 21st century.

I knew of Lemmel. Rosa and Donald's youngest child attended the school, known for its discipline, academic rigor, and involved parents: "These are the parents the intellectuals erase in their treatises on black pathology. But I saw them in effect at Lemmel" (Coates, 2009, p. 38). Although Lemmel's students came from a wide variety of economic and familial circumstances, the school was outstanding: "all the chaos of West Baltimore swirled around it but never inside. The school's guardians believed in the vocabulary of motivation and self-help" (Coates, 2009, p. 39). Lemmel's academic tracts were named for Black heroes and heroines such as Harriet Tubman, Booker T. Washington, Carter G. Woodson, and Thurgood Marshall. By his own admission, Coates was not the best student in the gifted tract. In his last year at Lemmel, he aimed to enter Baltimore Polytechnic, a selective public school known as "Poly." During his last year at Lemmel, he did well enough to gain admission.

But Poly's students were not immune to the temptations of the street and Mondawmin Mall,[6] which I recall as a shopping space whose merchants changed from purveyors of wares for strivers with middle-class aspirations to a mall that catered to clientele whose choices reflected the emerging hip-hop culture.

*   *   *

For Ta-Nehisi Coates, hip-hop was his bridge to Consciousness. Hip-hop woke him up, not quite in the way that his father would explain, but in a way that spoke to his son's generation. "That was the summer of 1988—the first great season of my generation. The Grand Incredible was dead, KRS converted to Consciousness and assumed the sentinel pose of Malik Shabazz. All the world's boom boxes were transformed into pulpits for Public Enemy" (Coates, 2009, p. 104). My daughter Alana Murray (2011), a contemporary of Ta-Nehisi Coates, explained her own experience of linking what she had learned in her inner-city childhood with what she was learning through hip-hop.

> In elementary school I attended Bunker Hill, a predominantly African-American public school in Washington, DC Bunker Hill was an outstanding school where teachers nurtured my knowledge of African-American history through assemblies, book reports and comprehensive lessons on the black experience. For example, my gym teacher, Mr. Lewis, loved and respected the artist-activist Paul Robeson. Our celebration of Mr. Robeson, a prominent African-American whose legacy was tarnished during the McCarthy era, took place in the backdrop of Reagan era Cold War politics. The school worked in partnership with my home to nurture my growing love for history.
>
> However, my experiences in [suburban] middle school and high school were far different. The middle school I attended was racially mixed and my high school was predominantly white. In these settings, my experience with the narrative of social studies and history was one of invisibility. With the exception of the discussion of slavery, Harriet Tubman, Rosa Parks and Martin Luther King, my teachers were silent on the role of people of color in history. As a student of color who loved history, I felt disassociated from the content of my classes. In fact, at times my teachers made me feel angry and disempowered because they would distort facts about African-American history and culture.
>
> In late adolescence I experienced a renaissance of my love for the history of people of color. One of the unique aspects of growing up as a member of

the Generation X period in hip-hop was the knowledge generated by Public Enemy, Poor Righteous Teachers, Queen Latifah, De La Soul and other hip-hop groups whose music had a distinctly Afrocentric flavor. The music of the late 1990s inspired me to study a past which had been muted during my high school years.

For many Black suburban children, the school, the media, and peers—rather than the home and neighborhood people and places—were the primary sites of learning. In the Washington, DC, neighborhood where my children attended school, we parents could walk with children the two blocks to the business district, and sometimes we formed a series of parent checkpoints to watch our children on the walk to school. We wanted to give them the experience of independence (if not the reality) on streets that might prove dangerous.

Most suburban neighborhoods were not "walkable." Although Columbia had been designed with interconnected walking path in "villages" with distinct features, when my children were teenagers, we lived in the sparse developments that surrounded the town. Young people complained constantly that there was no "place" to go. Buses and minivans were predominant modes of transport, even for kids who participated in extracurricular clubs, sports, and other activities. Kids hung out in their bedrooms or family rooms, watching TV, playing video games, listening to music, or reading. My children, including my stepson Kobie and my daughters (Kali and Alana) frequently welcomed to our home other teens and the occasional younger brother, sister, or cousin. Our house was a block from the school; other parents and I would monitor in person or by phone. For the group who gathered to eat leftovers, kick around a soccer or football in the yard, watch TV, and do homework, it was a safe place, a break from the "programming" (from soccer to community service to after-school projects) whose goals were worthy, but left no time unfilled or unaccounted for in a child's life.

*   *   *

The Coates and Murray stories address two important aspects of the adjustments that children have to negotiate in schools. The first is academic, which includes a wide range of skills and outcomes, such as reading, mathematics, performance on standardized tests, and grades. The second is social and emotional behavior. This includes attitudes toward school, observance of rules, internalizing and externalizing behaviors, motivation, social support, and delinquency. As Kathryn Wentzel (1999) points out in the overview of the important issue of *Educational Psychologist* on social influences, "If a child learns to engage in cooperative and prosocial interctions with others, to follow rules, and to strive to achieve standards for performance set by adults, they are more likely to succeed at school than children who do not" (p. 60).

The two stories also underline the importance of children's everyday experience, which Robin Moore and Donald Young (1978) specify as three interdependent realms: physical, or physiographic space, which includes objects, buildings, natural elements, and people; social space of human relationships; and psychological space, the realm of body and mind. Aspects of these environmental realms affect school adjustment of children at all socioeconomic levels.[7] For African American children, school adjustment can include bridging the cultures of home, school, and community. One approach to such mediation is the creation of culturally responsive classrooms. For African American children (compared to other children), this classroom environment requires an understanding of such behaviors as the greater use of social cues in the environment and the preference for cooperative versus individual interaction, as well as an understanding of how such cultural styles influence motivation, learning, and the selection of instructional strategies (Shade, Kelly, & Oberg, 1997).

In these days when global climate change is a subject for debate, we have become increasingly alarmed by how physical space affects school-related behavior. Consider environmental toxins, for example. Toxic chemicals are ubiquitous: mercury in fish; lead in plumbing, soil, and drinking water; pesticides on fruits and vegetables. What we don't know about the effects of environmental toxins far exceeds what we do know. According to the Collaborative on Health and Environment's Learning and Developmental Disabilities Initiative (2008), of more than 80,000 potentially hazardous chemicals, conclusive evidence for effects on the developing nervous systems exists for about 10 of them, with 3 of them—lead, PCBs (polychlorinated biphenyls), and mercury—studied most extensively. Upon reading the report of the Collaborative, one of my students in a graduate seminar I taught on environmental influences and school performance remarked,

> I was surprised by how little we know about the effects of chemicals on the human body or the infant body, for that matter. Just this past week, the news was talking about a possible link between a chemical used to make various plastic bottles and diseases or disabilities. Now each time I take a sip of water from a plastic bottle, I think, "Am I contaminating my body with one of these unknown 80,000 chemicals we just have not had the time or money to investigate thoroughly?

Gary Evans (2006) and the Collaborative on Health and Environment (2008) reviewed studies whose findings revealed that lead accumulation in grade school students is associated with deficits in IQ reading, learning, and memory. Mercury, which can pollute the water and food supplies, causes learning and developmental disorders. Even low levels of mercury are associated with reading and IQ deficits, among others, and PCB exposure also depresses IQ and reading ability. Toxins can also affect behavioral adjustment. For example, lead exposure is associated with ADHD and with increased hyperactivity and externalizing behavior.

Summaries of research (Anderson, 2004; Evans, 2006, National Research Council, 2006) reported excessive noise adversely affects memory and attention, speech perception, and reading comprehension. Excessive noise in and around the school building comes from aircraft, traffic, lawnmowers, sports, classrooms, and other sources. Karen Anderson (2004) writes that school personnel typically are unaware of the negative effects of excessive noise on students' academic performance. Another one of the graduate seminar students said, upon reading the National Research Council (2006) report, *Green Schools: Attributes for Health and Learning,*

> The readings increased my awareness of the importance of sound quality to a student's learning ability. As an adult, I am not able to hear all the distractions some of my students are struggling to separate as background noise versus knowledge noise. The fact that students are often suffering in poorly planned acoustic schooling environments is just one more reminder of the diverse types of support for students that should be acknowledged and fought for.

African American children in rural and urban areas face daily exposure to environmental hazards. Daria E. Neal (2008) discusses the major reason for this situation: historic and continuing discrimination in the United States, from the inability of African Americans to get mortgages, segregation in the housing market, and unfair decisions about land use. Neal writes,

> Limited housing opportunities for African Americans resulted in the creation of predominately African American communities located in the most environmentally toxic locations. Many African American communities are located in areas zoned for mixed residential/industrial/commercial use, while predominately white communities tend to be zoned strictly for residential use. (p. 1)

In addition to the effects of excessive noise and toxic pollution outside the school, many of the schools in African American neighborhoods are housed in deteriorating buildings.

Healthy schools in healthy neighborhoods are a major concern of the environmental justice movement that emerged in the late 1970s to combat environmental racism, which Brophy, Lopez, and Murray (2011) define as "any policy, practice, or directive that disproportionately affects the environment of individuals, groups, or communities based on race" (p. 161). The movement was a logical next step of the Civil Rights Movement; indeed many of its organizers were active in the ongoing Black freedom struggle. Leaders of the movement had been civil rights activists. Cora Tucker, for example, met informally with a small group of children in her Halifax, Virginia, basement. In 1975, when the group grew to 200, Tucker organized the children and adults into a grassroots organization called Citizens for a Better America (Engle, 1991). Its first action was building a recreational center for Black and White youth. In the mid-1980s, Tucker led a coalition to halt plans for a nuclear waste dump in her county (Cora Tucker (1938–1997), 1997).

Schools as Sites of Resistance

Many scholars make the important point that segregated African American schools, particularly in the South, were sites of resistance for those who sought racial justice through instruction in traditional academic subjects, social deportment, and the contributions of Black persons and communities (cf. Morris, 2004, for a summary of the scholarship of Black agency in educational institutions during legalized segregation and a study of schools that display agency in the post-Civil Rights era). Given the deteriorating and unhealthy buildings that house many schools, the ambient toxins that affect all of us, and students whose young lives may be affected by hazardous substances before they begin school on day one, schools that serve predominantly Black children have becomes sites of resistance for environmental justice and more traditional forms as well. At the turn of the 21st century, I witnessed this expanded mission of a school as a place in the network of learning in which African American children could see parents, teachers, and community members fighting for students to progress optimally, despite the adverse circumstances in the physical, social, and personal spaces.

* * *

The school building was in disrepair and its grounds unkempt when Frances Robinson began her duties as principal at the start of the school year in 1995. Just the semester before, *The Washington Post* had reported that Stanton Elementary School was one of 11 District of Columbia schools that had failed to pass fire code inspections. Ms. Robinson believed that the state of the building, built in the 1930s, was in part responsible for the flight of parents and students to other, more desirable places. "Based on what I had been looking at," she writes, "I could not blame them for their flight" (F. Robinson, 2000, p. 35).

As Ms. Robinson was assuming the duties of principal at Stanton, my colleagues and I at the Johns Hopkins/Howard University Center for Research on the Education of Students Placed At Risk (CRESPAR) set out to measure indicators of resilience and risk, and to identity patterns that characterized children who did well and even thrived despite the presence of stressful life events and perceived violence. I was to collect data at Stanton, one of three schools in the original study. The Stanton study soon expanded into a multifaceted effort in which I collected data as planned and also collaborated with Ms. Robinson and the faculty to apply principles derived from resilience research within the framework of the school's reform efforts. These efforts included districtwide instructional programs as well as enrichment activities that the school was conducting with "partners in education," including parents, churches, law firms, volunteers in government agencies, and community-based organizations.

Once the formal student data collection had ended in 1998, I remained as a partner in different roles: as judge for the science fair, as a professional development workshop designer and presenter, and "sounding board" for the principal. I also continued to collect information about the school, which led to an important discovery: the public image of the school was changing—it seemed to have more positive than negative elements.

I began to ask of the Stanton data, was it possible that Stanton had recast an existing narrative? If so, how? The importance of this question was heightened when I read of community psychologist Julian Rappaport's (2000) work with a school in a midwestern community, where he tried a variety of school-community programs. He writes,

> Programs is not the answer. What is needed is a new setting narrative that speaks of the talents, skills, and abilities of the students, their families and neighbors. Frankly, such a culture change is working against entrenched narratives that are believed by both the oppressors and oppressed. (p. 21)

I had visited schools like Stanton many times in my career. Some were in Anacostia, the same Washington, DC, neighborhood in which Stanton was located. Anacostia is a sprawling urban area east of the river of the same name. As a child, I had attended a school housed in a similar structure—brick, multistoried, with high ceilings—and with academic programs that resembled Stanton's, located in one of Atlanta's most poverty-stricken neighborhoods. Students were performing at the low end of the scale. Fights, some in which I was a participant, broke out in the halls, the bathrooms, and the busy street in front of the school. Apart from my experience, I carried images of urban schools gleaned from films about the "hood," research reports, newspaper articles, and popular books about the lives of inner-city children. Rappaport (2000) calls these societal images and the stories they convey *dominant cultural narratives.* Like stereotypes, these narratives are persistent and difficult to change. They are often at odds with the realities of individual schools, in Rapaport's words, the *community* or *setting narratives.* Equally as important, community narratives are shared among members of the community and serve as the context for the *personal stories.*

> Communities tell stories. Settings tell stories. Visual symbols index stories. People change stories even as they act within them. Even as individuals are shaped by the community narratives they are given, those very narratives can be reshaped by the people who receive them. (p. 7)

When I first arrived at Stanton in March 1996, I found a nearly perfect fit between the setting and stereotype. True, AmeriCorps volunteers had painted the cavernous hallways, and the custodial staff was keeping a constant vigil to stem the flow of water from leaking toilets and sinks. Volunteers had been recruited to paint the auditorium. Amid repairs and refurbishing, Ms. Robinson had begun to assemble resources for upgrading academic achievement.

The school had had an erratic academic history since the predominantly all-White neighborhood changed after the schools were integrated in the 1960s: the White population in Anacostia went from 82% in the 1950s to 14% in the 1970s. Courtland Milloy's article in the December 10, 1985, edition of *The Washington Post* describes the school's mostly poor and working-class students as scoring "at or better than the national average on standardized tests for several years" (p. C1), despite the lack of up-to-date textbooks and a deteriorating physical plant. When Ms. Robinson arrived, Stanton's academic program was, like the building, in a state of decline. At the start of the 1996–1997 school year, the district would designate Stanton as a targeted assistance school (i.e., one requiring program improvement to increase student achievement). The enrollment of slightly over 500 students was virtually all African American. Approximately 98% of the students were eligible for the free or reduced-price lunch program, and the median household income in the area from which the school drew its students was $12,000, an amount below the U.S. federal poverty guideline of $15,150 for a family of four in 1995 (Stanton Elementary School, 1996).

The social conditions in the neighborhood surrounding the school were cause for concern. According to the 1990 Census of Population and Housing, of individuals 18 years and older in the school's zip code, 35% had not graduated from high school, the unemployment rate at 10% was twice as high as the national average, and 31% of families with children under 18 lived below the poverty line. Violent crimes and drug use plagued the neighborhood. Indeed, we CRESPAR researchers had chosen the school because of its profile, its setting narrative.

Moving Into the Setting

I arrived at Stanton on the last Wednesday in March 1996. I was there to arrange for a longitudinal study to understand how children's educational resilience (or school adjustment) is influenced by neighborhood violence and life stress (called "vulnerability factors") and a protective factor—social support from family, peers, and teachers—hypothesized to reduce the effects of violence and stress. The plan was to conduct an initial survey of the third- and fourth-grade students using standard instruments to measure the varied signs of individual resilience, as well as the children's perceptions of stressors. Another assessment would be conducted the following year. Previous research had produced mixed results regarding the role of particular protective and vulnerability factors (Luthar, Cicchetti, & Becker, 2000), and I hoped our findings would illuminate the discrepancies.

Ms. Robinson warmed to the idea. She explained that her first priority was to improve students' reading and math skills. That emphasis was consistent with an assessment of resilience: children who function competently in the face of adversity can read and solve problems. She asked me to speak before parents and teachers, to gauge their interest in and willingness to approve the project, and further explained that a high proportion of the students had been exposed to drugs before they were born. She believed that poverty and household composition—many of the students were from single-parent homes—were also impediments. "What can you do to help the teachers deal with the conditions of the children's lives?" she asked.

I listened as Ms. Robinson spoke about things she was doing and wanted to do in the school. These items blended past and present. Some, like refurbishing of the physical plant and installation of computers, were in progress; others, like an all-male second-grade classroom, run military style, were barely outlines. I could see that the computers were there. We were meeting in a room filled with used computers, lined up neatly, unplugged, on the floor. I sensed that she would get to all the items on the list. Maybe it was her tone—authoritative but optimistic.

I still wondered, what does she think she can do in this place? On the day of our meeting, another negative event occurred. As *The Washington Post* reported, "2nd-grader stabs 5 others with found medical tools" in a field next to the school (Kyriakos, 1996). Ms. Robinson was appalled:

> During my first year as principal, my school made the news negatively—a principal's nightmare. A student had found lancets [small needles] on the community field on his way to school and used these needles to scratch a few classmates. The media blew the situation out of proportion and indicated that the possibility existed that the scratched students might be suffering from AIDS. I had no idea how anything positive could come out of that situation. Yet, the next day television crews came to the school to hear what I had to say. They went out of their way (most unusual for the media) to show what the little lancets resembled. However, columnist Cortland Milloy at *The Washington* Post, wrote an excellent article about Stanton, focusing on its programs and students, and focused on a first grade boy who was anchoring our school radio program. (F. Robinson, 2000, pp. 38–39)

I interpret this account as one example of how Ms. Robinson interrupted the public setting narrative, reframing it to highlight the school's assets. Despite this glimmer of good news, the intellectual and physical deterioration of Stanton, if not intractable, seemed arrested, waiting, if history had its way, for the next decline.

Becoming Partners

Although Stanton did not yet have a robust home-school partnership, the school was building on an existing base that included two churches, a community-based service agency, and volunteer groups. A long-standing partner was Project 2000, a program launched by Dr. Spencer Holland, which had mentored Stanton students through high school (Holland, 1996).

The school's vision statement, set forth in the annual Title 1 improvement plan for 1996–1997, highlighted the role of partners:

> The vision of the Edwin L. Stanton Elementary School is that it will serve as a beacon to this diversely talented school community, representing the highest standards of academic achievement and social deportment. Stanton will continue to forge partnerships that promote learning environments

where the achievement of World Class Standards will become a reality. The school envisions confident students who will exit this learning community with outcome-based experiences, ethical standards, intellectual curiosity, and perseverance; prepared to perform competitively in a technological, global society. (Stanton Elementary School, 1996, p. 1)

Shadowing this hopeful vision was a complex reality. Already the needs statement referred to the "resilient urban child who is impacted by influences outside of the school which are brought into the school." A resilience narrative was becoming a part of the school's vision. But the document drew a dismal picture of one group of students: "Too many are substance abuse infected and affected children.... Teachers observe their uncontrollable behavior, hyperactivity, and learning disabilities. While they feel somewhat unprepared to meet their needs, they are making every effort to do so" (pp. 7–8).

Against that backdrop, late in August 1996, the faculty and Ms. Robinson came to Howard University's School of Law campus for a staff development retreat. The one-day retreat was more like a seminar among colleagues than a formal workshop. There were no handouts; neither was there an evaluation. We covered topics suggested by the faculty and Ms. Robinson and talked about student motivation, discipline, substance abuse, and neighborhood violence in the language of risk, resilience, and protection. In one of the three sessions, for example, we used Benard's (1991) threefold categorization of protective factors (high expectations, opportunities for participation, and caring and support) to brainstorm concrete examples in the Stanton school and neighborhood and in children's families. Throughout the workshop, teachers expressed the need for Stanton's students to have opportunities beyond their neighborhood. One teacher's comment was representative: "Our students must not be locked into Southeast as their world. They must recognize their heritage and stand tall. Our world is made up of a very diverse population. They must give respect and demand respect" (Field notes, August 2, 1996). One discovery that we made in the session was the school indeed had created opportunities for students to explore the world beyond their neighborhood, but only a handful of students in each grade had participated. We set a goal to involve as many students as possible in classroom activities, extracurricular clubs, and special events.

After the retreat, the school year started, and my research assistants began the surveys in all grades but the kindergarten and first. Throughout the school year, Ms. Robinson and I met often. In her office with high ceilings and African artifacts, we reviewed the programs that the school had attempted in recent years. The school, like other schools that I had studied in my work, had many remnants of programs, components remaining from reforms never fully implemented or tried for a year or two with special funding that had ended. Also, the school had programs in the vestigial stages. Examining the vestiges and remnants, Ms. Robinson identified her most urgent need: a child development specialist who could work with troubled children and their parents. Together, we searched for and found a recent doctoral graduate, who was hired part-time. We talked about ways to fill gaps in other programs, identifying contributions that community partners could make. Ms. Robinson asked me to search the literature for school programs for use with students who came from families in which drug use was prevalent. The resulting books and articles were the nucleus of a small collection of resources, housed in the library, for teachers to use.

*   *   *

Ms. Robinson considered her work to be a Christian ministry, one reminiscent of the role of Calvin Brown, the founder of the high school from which she graduated. Respecting the doctrine of separation between church and state, however, she did not use the language in her daily work, but in her memoir, she writes,

> If Dr. Brown, who was born in an era of slavery, was able to establish the first black high school in North Carolina before he was thirty years of age, what cannot we, who are educators born long after the Emancipation Proclamation was signed, accomplish in getting boys and girls of color to read, write, think, and speak literately? It must be noted also that such an endeavor necessitated funds that Dr. Brown did not personally possess. However, God placed men and women along the way to provide the financial backing for the first black school in North Carolina. (F. Robinson, 2000, pp. 17–18)

Ms. Robinson believed that spirit-inspired

> principals, teachers, educational aides, partners-in-education, maintenance, office, and cafeteria workers can work in any situation and go anywhere when they know that where God sends them, He equips them to have never-ending victories. . . . With an unfaltering faith, educators can challenge children to conceive and dream the impossible. (F. Robinson, 2000, p. 33)

Moreover, she writes, "God promised me that Stanton would be turned around and be recognized across the country" (p. 35).

I interpret Ms. Robinson's confidence in her own success and that of others as one key to the loyalty and generosity of community partners. Throughout the year, I had observed community partners—themselves a diverse group in terms of race/ethnicity and employment—in essential roles. "Book Buddies" from the Pentagon read to first graders. A community-based program provided mentoring for 35 girls in the fifth and sixth grades. A church partner arranged for General Colin Powell to speak at a school assembly. A coalition of African American professionals organized 90 volunteers to wire every classroom and office for the Internet. At a year-end awards ceremony, the PTA president, the assistant principal, and Ms. Robinson recognized 18 community partners. Virtually all the students had received direct benefits from them.

Despite the efforts of the school faculty, the parents, and the community partners, the results of the spring tests were mixed. For example, in reading, a substantial majority of first graders (80%) scored at the basic level and above on the Stanford 9, but 58% of the second graders scored below basic. In mathematics, 80% of the third graders were at the basic level and above, however, fifth graders were almost evenly split with 54% below basic and 46% at basic or above. The 1997–1998 update to the school's improvement plan (Stanton Elementary School, 1997) placed literacy as the first priority, with the goal of ensuring that every child would be reading on grade level by the end of the school year. Improvement in mathematics was a close second. The plan to reach these goals included participation in a national trial of a reading program for first graders, contracting with a private provider of reading instruction for third graders and tutoring—provided by community partners—for children in other grades. Other partners were continuing activities from the prior year and planning new initiatives.

As my collaboration with Ms. Robinson deepened, I realized that the school's actions to increase resilience would have to become part of the story. The student data would not be understandable without the emerging setting narrative. Parts of the student story—albeit told in group averages and standard deviations—and the school narrative were in dynamic interaction. But I had trouble starting on the expected technical report for Hopkins. The school was not relying on a "magic bullet," but was carefully choreographing the old and new efforts of the entire school toward a vision that highlighted student achievement and confidence. In this day of "brand name" programs developed by leading researchers and administrators, this approach of using available resources would, we thought, probably be of little interest. But, for the record, Ms. Robinson and I decided to co-author a technical report that told the Stanton story.

*   *   *

The 1997–1998 academic year began far from the city, at a rustic conference center in the hills and pastures of Northern Virginia. A community partner had underwritten the retreat for faculty and parents who were part of the school's staff. A consultant was present to facilitate the discussions of the actions needed to implement a systemwide instructional initiative, and I was invited to present the results of the student surveys. The agenda was designed to prepare the faculty for the fall administration of the Stanford 9 and to inspire confidence and positive attitudes. A cookout and hayride punctuated the otherwise serious discussions and presentations.

I distributed a handout that summarized how Stanton students rated themselves. Overall, the students perceived themselves as capable and proud of the way they were. Children thought they got along well with parents, liked them, and experienced parental acceptance and approval. On the dimensions of self-concept, ability, enjoyment, and interest in reading and math ranked high, and the number one motivation for reading among the students was the importance of reading. The students felt they could rely on the teachers, their peers, and most of all, their parents, for support. We discussed the results, which were comparable to those of normative samples, and agreed that the children in the study could draw on several kinds of resources to help them overcome adversity.

The school year followed a predictable schedule: districtwide testing on the Stanford 9 in the fall and spring, daily instructional activities, school assemblies, field trips, a Parent Academy, and the creation of extracurricular activities. Ms. Robinson used opportunities to communicate the school's vision. She stressed the need for writing and other forms of literacy:

> Standards must be set and assessed. I am not happy viewing sloppy writing that does not represent the best that children can do. Students should also read books outside of their class work. They should check books out of the library, be given book reports to do, and receive written or verbal feedback. (Stanton Elementary School, 1997, p. 3)

She and the teachers encouraged students to express themselves:

> The recognition of the school is increasing the self-esteem and importance of parents, students, and the staff of the school.... four students entered the United Black Fund's annual citywide essay contest, "I Love Life and I Want to Live" in song, essay, and poster. Two students won first place in the essay contests. Another student won second place for the poster entry, and one teacher's entire third grade class won third place in the original song composition. (F. Robinson, 2000, pp. 42–43)

At the Partnership Summit in March 1998, an event celebrating the efforts of community partners, she said, "Children should be able to read, write, speak, think and feel good about themselves." The partners had contributed to achieving the vision by providing regular tutoring and mentoring, implementing a Rites of Passage program, donating computers, providing training in peer conflict resolution, and donating resources.

During the summer of 1998, Ms. Robinson and I completed our technical report, *Exploring the Dynamics of Resilience in an Elementary School* (Nettles & Robinson, 1999). It described how the school was using two principles underlying resilience to improve the school: increasing available resources and mobilizing protective processes of high expectations, opportunities to participate, and caring and support. It reported significant gains school-wide in reading and mathematics. We concluded,

> Resilience is emerging as an organizing principle that gives Stanton a means of integrating school improvement, regular and enhanced curricular offerings, and processes that emphasize caring, high expectations, and opportunity. . . . We do not view this as another program to improve test scores and grades, although the results thus far are promising. Rather, we see this as a way of giving meaning to the phrase, "building on children's strengths." (Nettles & Robinson, 1999, p. 18)

The report described a school in the midst of a changing narrative and that change was positive and palpable.

Practicing Cultural Sensitivity

Choreographers, like school principals, have a vision, and they plan the steps that will realize the vision. In her role as principal of Stanton, Ms. Robinson linked the widely held goal of academic achievement for inner-city children with a parallel, divinely inspired vision of recognition of the school's accomplishments. Although she promoted classroom-level planning processes, she continually reviewed and revised schoolwide plans. She came from similar circumstances as her students; like them, she had attended a virtually all-Black school with Black teachers and leadership. She had achieved success in academic settings—she was a role model. She had the skills to support and encourage others, as her interactions with community partners indicated.

This picture is consistent with research that identifies empowering community settings with leadership that is inspirational, shared, talented, and committed (Maton & Salem, 1995). Ms. Robinson also shows characteristics of psychological empowerment. I interpret her critique of easy acceptance of externally generated theory and research as one piece of evidence of her critical awareness (Perkins & Zimmerman, 1995). Perhaps most empowering of all, she wrote her own story and encouraged the students to tell their own—in writing, painting, designing science projects, and other ways. With community partners-in-education, Ms. Robinson and the faculty created a setting that students viewed as supportive and provided students with opportunities to participate in valued roles and activities. Again, this is consistent with research on the characteristics of empowering community settings (e.g., see Maton & Salem, 1995).

After my role ended, Project 2000, a community partner, and Stanton students discussed strides made in academic achievement of Black boys on the November 16, 1999, broadcast of *Nightline*, and the report that Ms. Robinson and I wrote was published in a guidebook on resilience for educators (Nettles & Robinson, 1999). Ms. Robinson has retired, but still volunteers in the community. I have moved to another part of the country, but I follow Stanton via the Internet.

Into the New Century

As I write, the Great Recession, the first deep economic downturn of the 21st century, is the hardest of times since the depression of the 1930s. Poverty is widespread, especially among children. In 2011, according to Vanessa Wight, Michelle Chau, and Yumike Aratani (2011) of the National Center for Children in Poverty, the percentage of children in poor families stood at 21%; of all race/ethnic groups, the percentage was highest among Black children at 36%. Although Du Bois predicted that my generation—the Baby Boomers—would win the "big fight" for human rights, the challenges that Du Bois and his peers identified still remain, albeit in altered and in some cases, greatly intensified forms. Among them are poverty and the great divide between those who are wealthy and those less so, competition for diminished resources, continuing unemployment, environmental hazards, and changing directions for education in a technology rich world and the consequent need for continuous learning at every life stage.

Now and again, the educational, economic, and health conditions of all children draw the attention of practitioners, decision makers, and researchers. Although there are many community-based programs and projects for African American and other minority children, especially those in poverty, as in the 1950s and 1960s, increased civic participation is part of solutions to address disparities in children's access to education, health care, and social services. Having explored the experiences of African American children and the actions of determined parents and grassroots educators in communities, I turn to a reflection on how existing learning spaces can be enhanced and new ones created through neighborhood networks of lifelong learning.

Notes

1. *The Brownies Book* may be found online in the digital collections of the Library of Congress and at www.DuBoisopedia

2. Samuel Williams. Sermon. "October 18, 1959, Topic: Giving." Box 19, Folder 37. S. Williams Collection, Archives/Special Collections. Robert W. Woodruff Library, Atlanta University Center, Atlanta, Georgia.

3. Samuel Williams. Sermon. "Matthew 9:34ff, Providence 315/58. What is it That Makes One Truly Great?" Box 20, Folder 36. S. Williams Collection. Archives/Special Collections. Robert W. Woodruff Library, Atlanta University Center, Atlanta, Georgia.

4. Samuel Williams, Sermon. May 12, 1968, topic: "The Home as Environment." Box 19, Folder 50. S. Williams Collection. Archives/Special Collections. Robert W. Woodruff Library, Atlanta University Center, Atlanta, Georgia.

5. From "College Here We Come," Gray led the resident council to create a non-profit corporation through which the tenants managed their own housing. The Kenilworth-Parkside Management Corporation organized GED classes, after-school programs for children, and contracted for services (such as catering and repairs) with businesses that residents created. Before her death in 2000, she co-founded the National Association of Resident Management Corporations in 1988 and served as its board chairwoman (Estrada, 2000).

6. Mondawmin, which was built in the late 1950s, was one of the first indoor malls in the United States, but by the 1980s it reflected the increasing crime and physical decline of the area that began after the 1968 riots (Marx, 2007). The Mall was a couple of blocks away from my inlaws. Rosa Murray, my short, slender, and gregarious mother-in-law, walked to the mall to buy groceries and other things—she never learned to drive. On one of those walks in the 1970s, an adolescent male accosted her. A retired elementary teacher for the Baltimore City Schools, she beat him off with her purse before recognizing him as one of former students and calling him by name. The attempted mugging ended, the kid apologized, and left the scene.

7. Several theoretical perspectives guide the research on environmental effects on school adjustment. Although Bronfenbrenner's (1979) theory underlies much of the work on environmental influences on child outcomes, as Gary Evans (2006) noted, Bronfenbrenner's framework ignores "the physical context of human development even though many of the underlying processes that connect context to development are similar for physical and psychosocial environmental factors" (p. 423).

4

Necessary Spaces

The invention of the World Wide Web was nearly two decades in the future (Cailliau, 1995) when cultural critic Ivan Illich proposed in 1971 that resources for learning should be distributed through networks instead of schools. Following Illich, Christopher Alexander and colleagues (1977) used the term "network of learning" for the decentralization of educational systems. This network was to be in city spaces and places

> congruent with the urban structure itself. People of all walks of life come forth, and offer a class in the things they know and love: professionals and workgroups offer apprenticeships in their offices and workshops, old people offer to teach whatever their life work and interest has been, specialists offer tutoring in their special subjects. (p. 101)

The network metaphor is now applied to a variety of configurations from online learning to institutions such as libraries and museums, to communities of practice.

Necessary Spaces, pages 87–99
Copyright © 2013 by Information Age Publishing
87

Contemporary learning networks may incorporate supplementary education or complementary education. Professor Edmund Gordon and colleagues (Gordon, Bridglall, & Meroe, 2005) developed the concept of supplementary education, assuming that "high achievement is closely associated with exposure to family- and community-based activities and learning experiences that occur both in and out of school in support of academic learning" (p. ix). Proponents of complementary education seek to foster "a network of linkages" among institutions that offer high-quality, out-of-school programs whose goals for academic achievement are aligned. The Harlem Children's Zone (2010) and the Chicago Child-Parent Centers (Promising Practices Network, 2013) are examples. Building on these models, the Duval County (Florida) Public Schools and the University of North Florida are implementing Neighborhood Learning Networks in Jacksonville (Florida Institute of Education, 2012).

Many networks are in large cities where technological expertise and institutional partnerships are in varied stages of implementation. One example is the HIVE Learning Network, "a community of civic and cultural institutions dedicated to transforming the learning landscape, and creating opportunities for youth to explore their interests in virtual and physical spaces" (www.hivelearningnetwork.org/about/mission). At this writing, Chicago and New York are participating in the development of this new form of learning (made possible by digital media and called "connected learning"), which encourages youth to gain intellectual skills through interest-based learning and collaboration among peers. The MacArthur Foundation's Digital Media and Learning Initiative, DePaul University, and Mozilla support the HIVE Learning Network. The MacArthur Foundation also supports the Digital Media and Learning Research Hub (www.dmlcentral.net), which includes a blog, original research projects, a collection of resources, and an annual conference.

In seeking goals of effective learning and educational equity, the spatial and virtual approaches such as the ones just cited attempt to coordinate informal, nonformal, and formal learning activities among various institutional or social groups. With resources from foundations, governments, and individuals, experts (educators, designers, artists, and scientists) often play a role in creating the conditions for alignment of groups, activities, and goals. Moreover, these current reforms offer useful alternatives to stimulate innovation (such as the use of digital media) and improvements in networks of learning for the 21st century and also provide well-researched and designed ways to increase competence among children and adults in community settings.

But in my view, such approaches lack a critical component: a theoretical and practical account that communities themselves can use to develop sustainable roles in supporting children's behavioral and academic adjustment to schools. Amid all of the competing claims for approaches that will address the gaps in achievement and attainment of African American students, especially those in poverty, my vision is for the interconnection of grassroots, academic, and service resources in networks for lifelong learning in African American communities. I would ground such networks in four critical elements. The first is an educational philosophy, which I will describe below. The second aspect would be formal (school-like), nonformal, and episodic encounters and activities to foster necessary spaces: experiences that emerge from the child's holistic interaction with physical and social environments. Such experiences have a basis in culture as well as in current research on optimal development of African American children. Redundancy is the third, crucial feature. Explicit strategies must be developed for identifying and assuring that every child (not just the ones who attract attention for their qualities, be they social, physical, or intellectual) has one or more back-up resources, not only for material needs but for experiential requirements as well. Finally, the learning experiences of adults in the community would be highlighted so that children could see that there is no distinction between living and learning.

In concluding this narrative exploration of the physical, social, and personal spaces in Southern and other communities, I offer what I have learned about how "networks of learning" have been influential in the past. I then take "necessary spaces" and other aspects of collective memory as a resource for grassroots restoration of networks that promote equality of educational opportunity and equitable educational outcomes for African American students.

Network Places and People as Resources for Success in Schools

After I examined autobiographical memories, I appreciated a richer legacy than the one I understood as a child. Especially before *Brown v. Board*, the 1954 Supreme Court holding, interconnection among the growing number of network places and people was strong; the clear and tight boundaries of Black neighborhoods and the restricted geographic landscape made for intimate relations among neighbors and diversity among occupations and economic circumstances. Legal and de facto denial of education opportunity and stereotypes about the intellectual capacity of Black students were major impediments to achievement of aspirations. Despite these barriers, networks of learning in African American communities (especially during the era of segregation in the U.S. South between 1870 and the 1950s) routinely generated and managed resources that contributed to children's desire for educational and occupational attainment.

What are the family and community resources associated with academic achievement? Building on Pierre Bourdieu's (1986) idea that academic achievement is associated with education-related assets (or "capital"), in addition to financial capital, Edmund Gordon (2002) cites five types: health, social, human, political, and cultural. Cornelia Flora and her colleagues (Emery, Fey, & Flora, 2006) include natural and built capital in a similar account, the Community Capitals Framework. This is a conceptual tool used to "mobilize resources within the community to address a variety of issues and to expand opportunities for children, families, schools, businesses, and other organizations" (Flora, Flora, Fey, & Emery, 2006, p. 1).

Social capital refers to the individual's interaction in personal and institutional networks of friends, contacts, and colleagues. These relationships inspire mutual aid and trust, which in turn, get things done (such as a job referral or access to persons within government systems). Robert Putnam (1995) includes the family as a potent, fundamental form of social capital. Several of the studies of neighborhood effects over the past three decades show that children in neighborhoods with high social capital and *human capital* (benefits such as knowledge and competences derived from education and training) also show positive outcomes on behavioral and academic adjustment to school (Nettles, Caughy, & O'Campo, 2008; Woolley et al., 2008).

In the essays in this collection, autobiographical writers described family members and their connections to social networks in the neighborhood, church, or places of employment and family willingness to engage networks on behalf of children. Before the 1960s, many Black neighborhoods (such as my own neighborhood of Washington Park in Atlanta) were occupationally and economically diverse. Children interacted with adults who had attained different types and levels of education; these adults modeled possible futures, however limited, while encouraging the young to go beyond what they saw each day.

Polity capital reflects participation and the sense of belonging to the social group; however, some definitions use the term "political capital" to include civic participation as well as access to power, power brokers, and resources (Flora et al., 2006). During the Civil Rights Movement, African American communities effectively used many strategies (such as boycotts of businesses, sit-ins, and nonviolent resistance) to influence how educational and other resources are allocated.

Natural capital refers to the community's natural assets: weather, water, soil, air quality, location, amenities (such as parks). Networks of learning—even those in the poorest neighborhood—had outdoor spaces in which children could play games and sports. *Built capital* includes buildings (houses, schools, libraries, and stores), and systems for communication and transportation, and the way these components are arranged. Until the middle of the 20th century, social capital in Black communities was facilitated, for example, by safe routes by which to walk to different destinations. "Walkability" of neighborhoods encouraged casual, face-to-face interactions and adult supervision of children.[1] Urban renewal in the 1950s and 1960s, which destroyed much of the built fabric in Black communities, also decimated social networks. For example, at a recent conference, I gave a talk about the network of learning. An African American colleague came over and said, "We're standing in the spot where my boyhood church once stood." The church and nearby business and houses had been destroyed, replaced by an interstate highway, parking lots, and a classroom building for the state university system.

Health capital refers to various aspect of the individual's physical and emotional condition (for instance, statements about overall health, energy level, and feelings of well-being). In African American networks of learning, exploring and playing in safe outdoor spaces conferred health benefits, and the presence of settlement houses and community centers provided additional spaces for recreation. Physicians' offices, health clinics, schools, and hospitals in the Black community were sites for parental learning about health practices.

Cultural capital has many meanings. Among them are African Americans' contributions of resources (time, money, and materials) in support of educational, social, and cultural institutions (Franklin, 2002); and individuals' use of powerful cultural symbols (in the form of behaviors, preferences, and attitudes) to gain status in the dominant, or mainstream social groups (Bourdieu, 1986). Carter (2003) argues that in addition to social behavior recognized by the dominant culture, low-income Black youths also invest time and energy into social behavior to gain status into nondominant groups; Carter views these two competing forms of behavior as dual cultural capitals: dominant and nondominant.

A key aspect of cultural capital is the African American philosophy of education. Theresa Perry (2003) contends that from their "collective experience with learning and education," (p. 12) a philosophy of schooling and education was developed in African American communities. This philosophy was handed down through the generations in stories, both oral and written. When Perry examined African American slave and contemporary narratives (including those of Frederick Douglass, poet Maya Angelou, and physicians Ben Carson and Joycelyn Elders), these personal stories consistently affirmed "the operative philosophy of schooling that has historically . . . supported the development and sustenance of effort optimism among African Americans as a historically oppressed group: education for freedom, racial uplift, citizenship, and leadership" (p. 63).

My essays suggest that community members lived this philosophy through their own learning activities (e.g., acquiring skill in leadership by participating in clubs and societies and competency in communicating with school staff about children's needs); through myriad acts that taught us to persist at tasks (such as learning to read or recite poetry); and through sermons and lessons that inspired service, hope for the future, and resistance to oppression. However, as Perry suggests, the African American philosophy of schooling is no longer transmitted in church, neighborhood, family, and other settings; African American children and youth no longer develop "identities of achievement." She writes,

> In the school, church, or community-based organization, this could involve organizing ongoing group activities for African-American youth that are intellectual in nature, including film clubs, literary societies, study groups, debating clubs, moot court competitions, African-American history and culture clubs, prelaw societies, and so on. (2003, pp. 101–102)

Intellectual groups would offer opportunities for practice, one of the "necessary spaces" I describe.

Building and Restoring Neighborhood Networks of Learning

Autobiographical memory includes events and images from individual experience. Seven experiences recur as environmental memories: connection, practice, empowerment, renewal, exploration, design, and resistance. I use the metaphor of "necessary spaces" to evoke both the place and the child's imaginative encounter (with persons and/or objects) from which these experiences emerge and to highlight the crucial role of such experiences in optimal child development. In the essays, I wove these autobiographical memories of African American childhood with findings from research and other sources into a shared recollection of experiences—collective memory—in networks of learning.

Through stories, writings, artifacts, drama, dance, and other representations, the community's memories can be shared, re-created, and passed on to the young. Cassandra Y. Johnson and J. M. Bowker (2004) argue that "collective memory involves the relaying or handing down of cultural history from generation to generation. Successive generations can be influenced by events that impact a nation, ethnic/racial group, or gender even though subsequent generations have no direct memory of such events" (p. 59). These authors describe how African American collective memories of the wilderness show ambivalence rooted in the experience of plantation life, sharecropping, and forest labor.

As applied to necessary spaces, for example, take collective memories of connection. Its myriad forms appeared in all the personal stories, and research underscores the importance of attachment to parents or other caregivers, attachment to prosocial institutions such as schools and positive peer groups, and to connections to ancestral heritage. The roots of African American collective memory of connection originate in many aspects of African life; in Clyde E. Chesney's review of literature (2008) for the Environmental Heritage of African-Americans Model, connectivity emerged as a theme. Chesney writes that

> As we travel, study and interact with our ancestral cousins, it does not take long to see the connectivity we have with Africans—400 years later. . . . African societies traditionally included the communal ownership of land; egalitarian character of village life; collective decision making; and extensive networks of social obligations. (p. 14)

In addition to intellectual groups, which Theresa Perry (2003) suggests offer opportunities for connection to peers and cooperative practice in mastering academic skills, "necessary spaces" and other aspects of shared environmental memories of past learning landscapes can be used to develop neighborhood capacity for renovating networks of learning. I offer three suggestions for educators in homes, schools, and communities.

* * *

First, "necessary spaces" can be used as conceptual tools for providing age-appropriate activities for African American children in the home and other neighborhood settings. For example, during the middle childhood years (ages 6 through 10), families can create resource maps for each child, with tags for each space (design, connect, empower, renew, practice, explore, resist) and opportunities to foster these types of experiences. To build self-efficacy in various areas, *practice* options for school-aged children might look something like this:

In the home, children participate in authentic adult tasks, such as monitoring healthy living using a family calendar, caring for a plant, doing household chores, playing board games about money, and reading books.

In the neighborhood, children participate in team sports; children work with adults on economic development and entrepreneurial projects; children use digital technologies in libraries, museums, and community technology centers.

When parents and caregivers visit schools, they talk with teachers about opportunities for practice (children have classroom time to work together cooperatively on learning tasks and engage in authentic writing tasks).

Parents and caregivers can look for children's *design* opportunities in the home, such as creating and performing poetry, problem solving about how space is used in the home (by, for example, choosing an area in which to do homework). Opportunities for *empowerment* (self-efficacy and sense of responsibility for others) can involve working with adults on community projects, such as elections, gardens, clean-up campaigns, and seasonal parties and parades.

For all necessary spaces, parents and caregivers can identify ways in which they can serve as coaches. They can, for example, create environments for children's practice; model civic participation (voting, going to school meetings, engaging in neighborhood watches, for example), and find ways and time to enhance their own learning and engage in learning tasks with children. Parents and caregivers with access to computers can use the virtual National Museum of African American History and Culture[2] as a resource. The Education and Tours section of the website shows, for parents, two broad sets of activities for family learning. The first, "Save Our African American History," can be used for the *connection* space. It shows an activity for recording family history through family members. The second set of activities is "Let Your Motto Be Resistance." Two of the activities in the *resistance* space include "You are the Photographer" and "Make Your Own Museum Exhibit"; these can also be used as *design* activities.

Educator lessons on saving African American history and resistance are available for teachers to use in classrooms. For example, a lesson in "Let Your Motto Be Resistance" challenges students in grades 3 through 6 to "take a stand." Teachers may also want to map necessary spaces for each of their students. Teachers can use the Engineering is Elementary project to integrate design activities into elementary science for grades 1 through

5. For example, the project includes storybooks that challenge students to solve an engineering problem faced by a child character. (The characters vary in race, ethnicity, or country. Other characters in the story include neighbors or relatives involved in engineering.) Students use the Engineering Design Process[3] to create a solution to the problem.

Many activities for teachers and other school personnel are found in the school-community partnership literature (e.g., Sanders & Sheldon, 2009; Trumbull, Rothstein-Fisch, Greenfield, & Quiroz, 2001). Some of the activities are designed to foster mutual learning interactions, such as the Personal Inventories for Educators and Parents reproduced in Sandra Christenson and Susan Sheridan's book, *Schools and Families: Creating Essential Connections for Learning* (2001). The inventories include questions about roles, interactions, and resources for student progress. These authors comment, "Beyond self-reflection, school personnel must be willing to learn not only *about* a family's uniqueness but also learn *with* and *from* them" (p. 78, emphasis in original).

Professionals and policy in different fields are already formulating approaches to improve the quality of children's everyday lives in neighborhoods and communities. The Committee on Environmental Health of the American Academy of Pediatrics (2009), for example, published a policy statement entitled, "The Built Environment: Designing Communities to Promote Physical Activity in Children." This document recommends that physicians ask patients and parents to identify places for physical and recreational activity and to offer suggestions for overcoming barriers to use and encourage patient and pediatrician advocacy for environmental improvements such as parks and playgrounds. Environmental psychologists and design professionals are exploring community-based efforts to create outdoor settings for healthy child development. Robin Moore and Clare Cooper Marcus (2008) urge us to include children in designing solutions:

> Middle-age children (definitions of outer limits vary, but roughly between 6 and 12) are skilled and capable of evaluating their surroundings and explaining their likes, dislikes, fears, and perceptions of territorial barriers (Moore, 1980)—and to make design proposals to improve their surroundings. (p. 153)

*   *   *

Second, collective memory of experience can contribute to the generation of education-related cultural resources in the built and natural environments. In addition to recollections of consequential events that occur in social spaces (such as families, neighborhoods and ethnic groups), physical surroundings play a role in collective memory of a group. As Maurice Halbwachs (1950) writes,

Each aspect, each detail, of this place has a meaning intelligent only to members of the group, for each portion of its space corresponds to various and different aspects of the structure and life of their society, at least of what is most stable in it. (p. 2)

The generation of built environment capital provides one example. Memories about physical structures can inspire social action to preserve learning spaces, such as museums, schools, and houses. As one of the volunteers for a collaboration of African American museums in southeast Georgia, I assist in various ways to support programming for children, youth, and other visitors. One of the museums is associated with Dorchester Academy, located in the rural town of Midway, Georgia, and one of the schools for freed people started in 1871 (at the urging of a former slave) by the American Missionary Society. Closed as a school in 1940, in the 1930s the Dorchester compound became a model for community action agencies; in the 1960s, it housed a store and a credit union, which helped finance housing and later conducted activities to increase civic participation, including voter registration and civil rights organizing. The boys dormitory is the only remaining structure of the old campus; the National Trust for Historic Preservation named the dormitory to the 2009 list of America's 11 Most Endangered Places. Tremendous community involvement, much of it from the adult children whose parents attended the school, has resulted in raising funds for preserving the structure, which remains the site for intergenerational celebrations (Dorchester Academy, 2013).

Three of the museums in the collaboration—the Beach Institute of African American Culture, the King-Tisdale Cottage, and the Ralph Mark Gilbert Civil Rights Museum—are housed on landmarks in Savannah's Black community. William Westley Law (1923–2002) led the effort to preserve these structures. Law grew up during the Depression in a poor family in Savannah, and his mother and grandmother instilled in him a love of reading and social justice. During his childhood, he attended the historic First African Baptist Church (instituted in 1777 and documented as the oldest continuous Black Baptist congregation in the United States). His pastor and mentor was Dr. Ralph Mark Gilbert, a leader in the Civil Rights Movement, who organized many branches of the NAACP across Georgia. Given his early interest in social justice and his mentor's influence, Law's subsequent activism is not surprising. When he was in high school, Law joined the NAACP Youth Council and later served as the President of Savannah State University's NAACP Youth Council. As an adult, he became a postman; he organized the Savannah-Yamacraw Branch of the Association for the Study of Afro-American Life and History; and, leading sit-ins, voter registration drives, and boycotts, he worked tirelessly to achieve civil rights for African Americans (Elmore, 2004).

Another aspect of his activism was preservation of African American sites of memory; as a preservationist, his projects followed his desire for social justice; his regard for his mentor, Dr. Gilbert; and his love for the Black community. When Law was President of the Savannah chapter of the NAACP, in 1993 he sought and received public funding to establish the Ralph Mark Gilbert Civil Rights Museum. The Museum was housed in the former Wage Earners Savings and Loan Bank building, constructed in 1914 in the heart of the Black business district by a Black contractor from Atlanta. Law implemented other projects, including acquisition of the Beach Institute, a school building erected in 1867 by the American Missionary Association and the Freedman's Bureau for the education of African American Children. The building is now known as the Beach Institute of African American Culture and houses collections of African American art.

* * *

Finally, memories of "coaches" in the neighborhood remind us of informal instructional processes that neighborhood residents used in that past. Beyond the long-standing use of coaching in sports and executive development, coaching is now a practice that is applied widely—from development of instructional skill in early language and literacy (Neuman & Cunningham, 2009) to prevention of alcohol and tobacco use among elementary school children (Botvin, Griffin, Paul, & Macaulay, 2003). Coaching can be a useful tool for building sustainable community development in the future. At the neighborhood or community level, there are guides to the coaching process that can be used to raise awareness about networks of learning and to stimulate community involvement for children. For example, Mary Emery, Ken Hubbell, and Becky Miles-Polka (2011) developed *A Field Guide to Community Coaching*, which details roles and strategies of coaching in six connected aspects of the community coaching process: readiness, relationship, results, reach (creating a positive mindset for goal attainment), reflection, and resilience. Ways to use the Community Capitals Framework mentioned above are included in the guide. As the authors point out, "The coach's role is not to do things for the community, but rather learn with community members about how to build their capacity to do things more effectively" (p. 11).

Memories of coaches can be used as examples of the supportive guidance and modeling that individuals provide in everyday social interactions with children, as well as the role of coaches in providing social and physical environments from which important experiences emerge. Images from the 2006 motion picture, *Akeelah and the Bee*, illustrate this point. Akeelah is an

11-year-old African American girl who attends a middle school in South Los Angeles. She is a bright girl, but avoids school and the reputation that she is a brainiac. She lives with her widowed mom and also her older brother, who occasionally engages with gangs. One night while watching television, she sees the National Spelling Competition. Her principal urges her to enter, she wins the school contest, and goes to the next level. The principal finds the required coach for her, who then takes her as far as he can, teaching her new words and how to use the English language.

Along the way, she encounters obstacles: balancing time with friends versus time for spelling practice, her mother's objections that Akeelah is neglecting her homework, other contestants' competitive parents, and her coach's decision to allow her to find her own way to succeed without his help. Throughout the film, Akeelah shows us what she learns from her spelling coach, her mom, and others beyond spelling to win: how to practice, how to connect with others through respect, empathy, and fair play; the empowering ingredients of self-efficacy and sense of responsibility to the community. She spends time with her girlfriends; the companions provide a space for renewal. She explores the city, taking the bus to a party in an unfamiliar neighborhood. Akeelah's progress through the competition becomes a source of pride for the community; a pivotal scene shows a network of learning in action. Network people—her mother, her brother, the postman, and other people in the neighborhood—in all of the neighborhood places (home, the streets, at school) are coaching Akeelah toward her dream.

Akeelah and the Bee is a film set in Los Angeles, one of the destinations to which African Americans took their cultural traditions during the Great Migration from the South. The 1982 photograph on the cover of this book captures another moment of children's experience. Smiling proudly, the children stand (two of them with hoes in hand) in front of a mural that depicts events in Black history. The building was the Anacostia Community Museum in Washington, DC, a museum of the Smithsonian Institution. According to a newsletter account,[4] the children had planted a garden in a vacant lot next to the museum and raised a variety of fruits and vegetables. They practiced basic science skills such as observation and classification, "and they enjoyed the satisfaction of actually seeing, *and tasting*, the results of their horticultural labors." Other images in the newsletter show a parent and Zora Felton, head of the museum's Education Department.

These images and the film are tangible reminders that people, places, and spaces for experience and action are components of neighborhood networks of lifelong learning that contribute to optimal development for children and the communities that support them.

Notes

1. Walkable neighborhoods are associated with not only health benefits (Frank et al., 2006), but contribute to the development of social capital (Rogers, Halstead, Gardner, & Carlson, 2011).

2. Construction of the Smithsonian National Museum of African American History and Culture building (NMAAHC) began in 2012 and is scheduled for completion in 2015. The virtual museum is up and running. The virtual NMAAHC (http://nmaahc.si.edu/) uses technology to capture stories about the experiences of ordinary American people. Stories are uploaded in text, audio, or visual images in the Memory Book. Memories are linked visually with museum holdings.

3. See the Engineering is Elementary website (www.mos.org/eie/index.php) for a description of the design process, the storybook, and other content.

4. "The children raised kale: A story of growing...and growing...from seed to maturity." (1983, March/April). *Art to Zoo: News for schools from the Smithsonian Institution, Off ice of Elementary and Secondary Education,* Washington, DC. Retrieved from http://www.smithsonianeducation.org/educators/lesson_plans/kale/atz_raisedkale_marapr1983.pdf

References

African American Historic Places/National Register of Historic Places. (1994). Washington, DC: National Trust for Historic Preservation.

Alexander, C., Ishikawa, S., & Silverstein, M. (with Jacobson, M., Fiksdahl-King, I., & Angel, S.). (1977). *A pattern language: Towns, buildings, construction.* New York, NY: Oxford University Press.

American Academy of Pediatrics. (2009). The built environment: Designing communities to promote physical activity in children. *Pediatrics, 123,* 1591–1598.

American Psychological Association Task Force on Resilience and Strength in Black Children and Adolescents. (2008). *Resilience in African American children and adolescents: A vision for optimal development.* Washington, DC: Author. Retrieved from http://www.apa.org/pi/families/resources/resiliencerpt.pdf

Anderson, J. D. (1988). *The education of Blacks in the South: 1860–1935.* Chapel Hill, NC: University of North Carolina Press.

Anderson, K. (2004). The problem of classroom acoustics: The typical classroom soundscape is a barrier to learning. *Seminars in Hearing, 25,* 117–129.

Annie E. Casey Foundation. (2010). *Early warning! Why reading by the end of third grade matters.* Retrieved from http://www.datacenter.kidscount.org/reports/readingmatters.pdf

Atlanta Regional Council for Higher Education. (2005). *Atlanta in the Civil Rights Movement: Direct action and desegregation (1960–1965).* Retrieved from http://www.atlantahighered.org/civilrights/essay_detail.asp?phase=3

Bae, L. (April 10, 2011). Why you've never heard of community action: Civic participation and poverty. *Harvard Political Review.* Retrieved from http://hpronline.org/united-states/civic-participation-and-poverty-look-ing-back-on-the-community-action-program/

Barbarin, O. (1981). Community competence: An individual systems model of institutional racism. In O. A. Barbarin, P. R. Good, O. M Pharr, & J. A. Suskind (Eds.), *Institutional racism and community competence* (pp. 6–19). Washington, DC: U.S. Government Printing Office.

Barton, C. E. (2001). Duality and invisibility: Race and memory in the urbanism of the American South. In C. E. Barton (Ed.), *Sites of memory: Perspectives on architecture and race.* New York, NY: Princeton Architectural Press.

BDPA Black Education and Technology Foundation. (2011). *The Dr. Jesse Bemley scholarship.* Retrieved from http://www.betf.org/scholarships/jesse-bemley.shtml

Bearden, R., & Henderson, H. (1993). *A history of African-American artists: From 1792 to the present.* New York, NY: Pantheon.

Becker, H. J. (1982). *Microcomputers in the classroom: Dreams and realities.* (Report No. 319). Baltimore, MD: Johns Hopkins Center for Social Organization of Schools.

Benard, B. (1991). *Fostering resiliency in kids: Protective factors in the family, school, and community.* Portland, OR: Western Center for Drug-Free Schools and Communities.

Berlin, I., Favreau, M., & Miller, S. F. (Eds.). (1998). *Remembering slavery: African Americans talk about their personal experiences of slavery and freedom.* New York, NY: New Press.

Berliner, D. C. (2005, August 2). Our impoverished view of educational reform. *Teachers College Record.* Retrieved from http://www.hub.mspnet.org/index/12043

Berrey, S. A. (2009). Resistance begins at home: The Black family and lessons in survival and subversion in Jim Crow Mississippi. *Black Women, Gender, and Families, 3,* 65–90.

Blassingame, J. W. (1979). *The slave community: Plantation life in the antebellum South.* New York, NY: Oxford University Press.

Borchert, J. (1980). *Alley life in Washington: Family, community, religion, and folklife in the city, 1850–1970.* Urbana: University of Illinois Press.

Botvin, G. F., Griffin, K. W., Paul, W., & Macaulay, A. P. (2003). Preventing tobacco and alcohol use among elementary school students through life skills training. *Journal of Child and Adolescent Substance Abuse, 12*(4), 1–17.

Bourdieu, P. (1986). The forms of capital. In J. Richardson (Ed.), *Handbook of theory and research for the sociology of education* (pp. 241–258). New York, NY: Greenwood.

Branch, T. (1988). *Parting the waters: America in the King years 1954–63.* New York, NY: Simon & Schuster.

Bronfenbrenner, U. (1979). *The ecology of human development.* Cambridge, MA: Harvard University Press.

Brooks, F. E. (n.d.). *Defining their destiny: The story of the Willow Hill School.* Portal, GA: Willow Hill Heritage and Renaissance Center.

Brophy, A., Lopez, A., & Murray, K. (Eds.). (2011). *Integrating spaces: Property law and race.* Austin, TX: Wolters Kluwer.

Brown, E. B., & Kimball, G. D. (1995). Mapping the terrain of Black Richmond. *Journal of Urban History, 21*(3), 296–346.

Cailliau, R. (1995). *A short history of the Web: Text of a speech delivered at the launching of the European branch of the W3 Consortium, Paris.* Retrieved from http://www.netvalley.com/archives/mirrors/robert_cailliau_speech.htm

Carter, P. L. (2003). "Black" cultural capital, status positioning, and schooling conflicts for low-income African American youth. *Social Problems, 50,* 136–155.

Cary, L. (1991). *Black ice.* New York, NY: Alfred A. Knopf.

Caughy, M. O., Nettles, S., & Lima, J. (2011). Profiles of racial socialization among African American parents: Correlates, context, and outcome. *Journal of Child and Family Studies, 20,* 491–502.

Caughy, M. O., Nettles, S. M., & O'Campo, P. J. (2007). Community influences on adjustment in first grade: An examination of an integrated process model. *Journal of Child and Family Studies, 16,* 819–836.

Caughy, M. O., Nettles, S. M., & O'Campo, P. J. (2008). The effect of residential neighborhood on child behavior problems in first grade. *American Journal of Community Psychology, 42*(1/2), 39–50.

Caughy, M. O., Nettles, S. M., O'Campo, P. J., & Lohrfink, K. F. (2006). Neighborhood matters: Racial socialization of African American children. *Child Development, 77*(5), 1220–1236.

Chase, H. (1994). *In their footsteps: The American Visions guide to African-American heritage sites.* New York, NY: Henry Holt.

Chawla, L. (1986). The ecology of environmental memory. *Children's Environments Quarterly, 3,* 34–42.

Chesney, C. E. (2008). African-American environmentalism: Issues and trends for teaching, research and extension. *Cooperative Extension Working Papers. Paper 1.* Retrieved from http://digitalscholarship.tnstate.edu/extension/4/

Christenson, S. L., & Sheridan, S. M. (2001). *Schools and families: Creating essential connections for learning.* New York, NY: Guilford.

Clandinin, D. J., & Connelly, F. M. (2000). *Narrative inquiry: Experience and story in qualitative research.* San Francisco, CA: Jossey-Bass.

Clark, K. B., & Clark, M. K. (1939). The development of consciousness of self and the emergence of racial identity in Negro preschool children. *Journal of Social Psychology, 10,* 591–599.

Clark, K. B., & Clark, M. K. (1947). Racial identification and preference in Negro children. In T. Newcomb & E. Hartley (Eds.), *Readings in social psychology* (Rev. ed., pp. 602–611). New York, NY: Henry Holt.

Coates, T. (2009). *The beautiful struggle: A father, two sons, and an unlikely road to manhood.* New York, NY: Spiegel & Grau.

Collaborative on Health and the Environment Learning and Developmental Disabilities Initiative. (2008). *Scientific consensus statement on environ-*

mental agents associated with neurodevelopmental disorders. Retrieved from http://www.healthandenvironment.org/initiatives/learning/about_lddi/activities

Compaine, B. M. (2001). Information gaps: Myth or reality. In B. M. Compaine (Ed.), *The digital divide: Facing a crisis or creating a myth?* (pp. 105–118). Cambridge: Massachusetts Institute of Technology Press.

Cone, J. H. (1991). *Martin & Malcolm & America: A dream or a nightmare.* Maryknoll, NY: Orbis.

Cooper Marcus, C. (1995). *House as a mirror of self: Exploring the deeper meaning of home.* Berkeley, CA: Conari.

Cora Tucker (1938–1997). (1997). *Southern Changes, 19,* 30–31. Retrieved from http://beck.library.emory.edu/southernchanges/article.php?id=sc19-2_008

Dorchester Academy. (2013). www.facebook.com/pages/Dorchester-Academy-Midway-GA/166327940095039

Du Bois, W. E. B. (1899). *The Philadelphia Negro: A social study.* Retrieved from http://archive.org/details/philadelphianegr001901mbp

Du Bois, W. E. B. (1920). The immortal child. In *Darkwater: Voices from within the veil.* Retrieved from http://etext.lib.virginia.edu/toc/modeng/public/DubDark.html

Du Bois, W. E. B. (1940). *Dusk of dawn: An essay toward an autobiography of a race concept.* New York, NY: Schocken.

Elmore, C. (2004). W. W. Law (1923–2002). *New Georgia Encyclopedia.* Retrieved from http://www.georgiaencyclopedia.org/nge/Article.jsp?id=h-2553

Emery, M., Fey, S., & Flora, C. (2006). Using community capitals to develop assets for positive community change. *CD Practice.* Retrieved from http://www.comm-dev.org/commdev/collection/2006%2013.pdf

Emery, M., Hubbell, K., & Miles-Polka, B. (2011). *A field guide to community coaching.* Retrieved from http://www.kenhubbell.com/pdfs/FIELDGUIDE-version-1final.pdf

Engle, C. (1991, Winter). *RPE* profile: Cora Tucker. *Race, Poverty & the Environment, 5.*

Epstein, J. L. (2001). *School, family, and community partnerships: Preparing educators and improving schools.* Boulder, CO: Westview.

Estrada, L. (2000, March 4). Public housing advocate Kimi Gray dies: Northeast woman a leader in converting projects to resident ownership. *Washington Post.*

Evans, G. W. (2006). Child development and the physical environment. *Annual Review of Psychology, 57,* 423–451.

Evans, M. D. R., Kelley, J., Sikora, J., & Treiman, D. J. (2010). Family scholarly culture and educational success: Books and schooling in 27 nations. *Research in Social Stratification and Mobility.* doi:10.1016/j.rssm.2010.01.002

Fields, M. G. (with Fields, K.). (1983). *Lemon Swamp and other places: A Carolina memoir.* New York, NY: Free Press.

Fisher, C. (2006). African Americans, outdoor recreation, and the 1919 Chicago race riot. In D. D. Glave & M. Stoll (Eds.), *"To love the wind and the rain": African Americans and environmental history* (pp. 63–76). Pittsburgh, PA: University of Pittsburgh Press.

Flora, C., Flora, J., Fey, S., & Emery, M. (2006). *Community capitals framework.* Retrieved from http://education.byu.edu/ellsymposium/documents/community_capital.pdf

Florida Institute of Education. (2012). *FIE/DCPS Title I Success by Design: PreK-3 Initiative: DCPS/FIE Neighborhood Learning Networks.* Retrieved from https://www.unf.edu/fie/FIE-DCPS_Networks.aspx

Frank, L. D., Sallis, J. F., Conway, T. L., Chapman, J. E., Saelens, B. E., & Bachman, W. (2006). Many pathways from land use to health: Associations between neighborhood walkability and active transportation, body mass index, and air quality. *Journal of the American Planning Association, 72*(1), 75–87.

Franklin, V. P. (2002, Spring). Introduction: Cultural capital and African American education. *The Journal of African American History, 175.*

Friendship Baptist Church. (n.d.). *85th anniversary.*

Fullilove, M. T. (1999). *The house of Joshua: Meditations on family and place.* Lincoln: University of Nebraska Press.

Georgia Department of Natural Resources. (2000). *Announcement of listing in the National Register of Historic Places.* Atlanta, GA: Kenan Research Center, Atlanta History Center.

Gilbert, C., & Quinn, E. (2000). *Homecoming: The story of African-American farmers.* Boston, MA: Beacon.

Gomez, M. A. (1998). *Exchanging our country marks: The transformation of African identifies in the colonial and antebellum South.* Chapel Hill: University of North Carolina Press.

Gordon, E. W. (2002, Winter). Affirmative development: Looking beyond racial inequality. *The College Board Review, 195,* 28–33.

Gordon, E. W., Bridglall, B. L., & Meroe, A. S. (Eds.). (2005). *Supplementary education: The hidden curriculum of high academic achievement.* Lanham, MD: Rowman & Littlefield.

Greenberg, C. L. (1991). *"Or does it explode?": Black Harlem in the Great Depression.* New York, NY: Oxford University Press.

Gruenewald, D. A. (2003). Foundations of place: A multidisciplinary framework for place-conscious education. *American Educational Research Journal, 40,* 619–654.

Gundaker, G. (Ed.). (1998). *Keep your head to the sky: Interpreting African American home ground.* Charlottesville: University Press of Virginia.

Halbwachs, M. (1950). Space and the collective memory. In M. Halbwachs (Ed.), *The collective memory.* Retrieved from http://web.mit.edu/allanmc/www/hawlbachsspace.pdf

Harlem Children's Zone. (2010). *The HCA project: 100 blocks, one bright future.* Retrieved from http://www.hcz.org/about-us/the-hcz-project

He, M. F., & Phillion, J. (Eds.). (2008). *Personal~passionate~participatory: Inquiry into social justice in education.* Charlotte, NC: Information Age.

Head Start. (1972). *Recommendations for a Head Start Program.* Retrieved from http://eclkc.ohs.acf.hhs.gov/hslc

High school boasts three eagle scouts. (1939, April 1). *Atlanta Daily World*, p. 1. ProQuest Historical Newspapers.

Hoffschwelle, M. S. (2006). *The Rosenwald schools of the American South.* Gainesville: University Press of Florida.

Holland, S. H. (1996). Project 2000: An educational mentoring and academic support model for inner-city African American boys. *Journal of Negro Education, 65*, 315–321.

hooks, b. (1990). *Yearning: Race, gender, and cultural politics.* Boston, MA: South End.

hooks, b. (2009). Belonging: A culture of place. New York, NY: Routledge.

Hughes, D., Rodriguez, J., Smith, E. P., Johnson, D. J., Stevenson, H. C., & Spicer, P. (2006) Parents' ethnic-racial socialization practices: A review of research and directions for future study. *Developmental Psychology, 42*, 747–770.

Hunter-Gault, C. (1992). *In my place.* New York, NY: Vintage.

Hurston, Z. N. (1984). *Dust tracks on a road: An autobiography.* Urbana: University of Illinois Press.

Hutchison, D. (2004). *A natural history of place in education.* New York, NY: Teachers College Press.

Illich, I. (1971). *A special supplement: Education without school: How it can be done.* Retrieved from http://www.nybooks.com/articles/archives/1971/jan/07/a-special-supplement-education-without-school-how-/

Jaynes, G. D., & Williams, R. M. (Eds.). (1989). *A common destiny: Blacks and American society.* Washington, DC: National Research Council.

Johnson, C. Y., & Bowker, J. M. (2004). African-American wildland memories. *Environmental Ethics, 26*, 57–75.

Johnson, H. B., & Hagerman, M. (2006, January). *Kids' talk about class divides: Privileged children's perspectives on social class inequality.* Paper presented at the annual meeting of the American Sociological Association, Montreal, Canada. Retrieved from http://www.allacademic.com/meta/p104804_index.html

Johnson, M. P., & Roark, J. L. (1984). *Black masters: A free family of color in the old South.* New York, NY: W.W. Norton.

Johnson, W. B. (1995). *Black Savannah, 1788–1864.* Fayetteville: University of Arkansas Press.

Journal of the National Medical Association. (1939). Charles William Powell. *JAMA, 31*(5), 226.

Kawachi, I., & Berkman, L. F. (Eds.). (2003). *Neighborhoods and health.* New York, NY: Oxford University Press.

Kerr, J., Rosenberg, D., Sallis, J. F., Frank, L. D., & Conway, T. L. (2006). Active commuting to school: Associations with environment and parental concerns. *Medicine & Science in Sports & Exercise, 38*(4), 787–793.

Kincheloe, J. L, & Pinar, W. (Eds.). (1991). *Curriculum as social psychoanalysis: The significance of place.* Albany: State University of New York Press.

King, W. (1995). *Stolen childhood: Slave youth in nineteenth-century America.* Bloomington & Indianapolis: Indiana University Press.

King, W. (2005). *African American childhoods: Historical perspectives from slavery to civil rights.* New York, NY: Palgrave Macmillan.

Kinloch, V. (2010). *Harlem on our minds: Place, race, and the literacies of urban youth.* New York, NY: Teachers College Press.

Kyriakos, M. (1996, March 30). *2nd grader stabs 5 others with found medical tools.* Retrieved from www.pqasb.pqarchiver.com/washingtonpost/search.html

Ladson-Billings, G. (2009). *The dreamkeepers: Successful teachers of African American children.* San Francisco, CA: John Wiley & Sons.

Levine, S. (2008). *School lunch politics: The surprising history of America's favorite welfare program.* Princeton, NJ: Princeton University Press.

Lewis, D. L. (2000). *W.E.B. Du Bois: The fight for equality and the American Century, 1919–1963.* New York, NY: Henry Holt.

Lewis, P. K. (1979). Axioms for reading the landscape: Some guides to the American scene. In D. W. Meinig (Ed.), *The interpretation of ordinary landscapes: Geographic essays* (pp. 11–32). New York, NY: Oxford University Press.

Luthar, S. S., Cicchetti, D., & Becker, B. (2000). The construct of resilience: A critical evaluation and guidelines for future work. *Child Development, 71,* 543–562.

Lyon, E. A. (2009). J. W. Robinson (1927–2008). In *The new Georgia encyclopedia.* Retrieved from http://www.georgiaencyclopedia.org/nge/Article.jsp?id=h-1075

Marshall, P. (2001). From the poets in the kitchen. *Callaloo, 24*(2), 627–633.

Martin, H. H. (1987). *Atlanta and environs: Volume 3: A chronicle of its people and events, 1940–1970s.* Athens: University of Georgia Press.

Marx, P. (2007). *Jim Rouse: Capitalist/idealist.* Lanham, MD: University Press of America.

Masten, A. S. (2001). Ordinary magic: Resilience processes in development. *American Psychologist, 56*(3), 227–238.

Mather, M., & Rivers, K. L. (2006). *The concentration of negative child outcomes in low income neighborhoods: A Kids Count/PRB Report on Census 2000.* Retrieved from http://www.aecf.org/upload/publicationfiles/census.pdf

Maton, K. I., & Salem, D. A. (1995). Organizational characteristics of empowering-community settings: A multiple case study approach. *American Journal of Community Psychology, 23,* 631–656.

McArthur, J., Hill, W., Trammel, G., & Morris, C. (2010). Gardening with youth as a means of developing science, work and life skills. *Children, Youth, and*

Environments, 20, 301–317. Retrieved from http://www.colorado.edu/journals/cye

McDonogh, G. W. (Ed.). (1993). *The Florida Negro: A Federal Writers' Project legacy.* Jackson: University Press of Mississippi.

McPartland, J., & Nettles, S. M. (1991). Using community adults as advocates or mentors for at-risk middle school students: A two-year evaluation of Project RAISE. *American Journal of Education, 99,* 568–586.

McPheeters, A. L. (1988). *Library service in black and white: Some personal recollections, 1921–1980.* Metuchen, NJ: Scarecrow.

Meier, A., & Lewis, D. (1959). History of the Negro upper class in Atlanta, Georgia, 1890–1958. *The Journal of Negro Education, 28*(2), 128–139.

Miles, M. B., & Huberman, A. M. (1994). *Qualitative data analysis: An expanded sourcebook.* Thousand Oaks, CA: Sage.

Milloy, C. (1985, December 10). D.C.school: Rich in spirit, cash poor. http://pqasb.pqarchiver.com/washingtonpost_historical/results.html?st=basic&uid=&MAC=50a23aa1f3f5c6104e90e36051420d61&QryTxt=courtland+milloy+D.C.+school%3A+rich+in+spirit&srtby=RELEVANCE&restrict=articles

Moffett, G. E., Weis, A. M., & Banilower, E. R. (2011). Engineering is elementary: Impacts on students historically-underrepresented in STEM fields. Retrieved from http://www.eie.org/content/articles-publications#2011

Moore, J. H. (Compiler). (1964). *Slaveowners census, Henry County, Georgia 1850.* Athens: University of Georgia. Retrieved from http://www.usgwarchives.net/ga/henry/census.htm

Moore, R., & Young, D. (1978). Childhood outdoors: Toward a social ecology of the landscape. In I. Altman & J. F. Wohlwill (Eds.), *Children and the environment* (pp. 83–130). New York, NY: Plenum.

Moore, R. C., & Cooper Marcus, C. (2008). Healthy planet, healthy children: Designing nature into the daily spaces of childhood. In S. R. Kellert, K. Heerwagen, & M. Mador (Eds.), *Biophilic design: The theory, science, and practice of bringing buildings to life* (pp. 153–203). Hoboken, NJ: Wiley.

Morris, J. E. (2004). Can anything good come from Nazareth? Race, class, and African American schooling and community in the urban South and Midwest. *American Educational Research Journal, 41,* 69–112.

Morris, J. E., & Monroe, C. R. (2009). Why study the U.S. South? The nexus of race and place in investigating Black student achievement. *Educational Researcher, 38,* 21–36.

Moss, T. (1998). *Tale of a sky-blue dress.* New York, NY: Avon.

Murray, A. D. (2011). *Countering the master narrative: Race, social studies, and the development of the alternative Black curriculum, 1890–1940.* Unpublished manuscript, College of Education, University of Maryland, College Park, MD.

Murray, C. A., Bourgue, B. B., Harner, R. S., Hersey, J. C., Murray (Nettles), S. R., Overbey, D., & Stotsky, E. S. (1980). *The national evaluation of the Cities in Schools Program* (Report No. 3: Program impact, (1978–79). Washington, DC: American Institutes for Research.

Murray (Nettles), S. R., Murray, C. A., Gragg, F. E., Kumi, L., & Parham, P. A. (1982). *National evaluation of the PUSH for Excellence Project: Final report.* Washington, DC: American Institutes for Research. (ERIC Document Reproduction Service No. ED240225)

Nathiri, N. Y. (Ed.). (1991). *ZORA! Zora Neale Hurston: A woman and her community.* Orlando, FL: Sentinel Communication.

National Park Service. (2012). *Gullah/Geechee: Cultural Heritage Corridor.* Retrieved from http://www.nps.gov/guge/faqs.htm

National Research Council. (2006). *Green schools: Attributes for health and learning.* Washington, DC: National Academies Press.

National Research Council and Institute for Medicine. (2002). *Community programs to promote youth development.* Committee on Community-Level Programs for Youth. J. Eccles & J. A. Gootman (Eds.), Board on Children Youth and Families, Division of Behavioral and Social Sciences and Education. Washington, DC: National Research Academy Press.

Neal, D. E. (2008). Healthy schools: A major front in the fight for environmental justice. *Environmental Law, 38,* 2. Retrieved from http://www.elawreview.org/elaw/382/healthy_schools_a_major_front.html

Nettles, S. M. (1991). Community involvement and disadvantaged students: A review. *Review of Educational Research, 61,* 379–406.

Nettles, S. M. (1992). *Coaching in community settings: A review.* Baltimore, MD: Johns Hopkins University, Center on Families, Communities, Schools, and Children's Learning. (ERIC Document Reproduction Service No. ED346083)

Nettles, S. M. (1999, April). *Coaching in community settings: Applications and outcomes.* Roundtable presentation at the annual meeting of the American Educational Research Association, Montreal, Canada.

Nettles, S. M., Caughy, M. O., & O'Campo, P. J. (2008) School adjustment in the early grades: Toward an integrated model of neighborhood, parental and child processes. *Review of Educational Research, 78,* 33–84.

Nettles, S. M., Mucherah, N., & Jones, D. S. (2000). Understanding resilience: The role of social resources. *Journal of Education for Students Placed At Risk, 5,* 47–30.

Nettles, S. M., & Robinson, F. P. (1999). Exploring the dynamics of resilience in an elementary school. In B. Cesarone (Ed.), *Resilience guide: A collection of resources on resilience in children and families.* Report No. 26. (ERIC Document Reproduction Service No. ED426172)

Neuman, S. B., & Celano, D. (2001). Access to print in low-income and middle-income communities: An ecological study of four communities. *Reading Research Quarterly, 36,* 8–26.

Neuman, S. B., & Cunningham, L. (2009). The impact of professional development and coaching on early language and literacy instructional practices. *American Educational Research Journal, 46,* 532–566.

Neverdon-Morton, C. (1997). The Black woman's struggle for equality in the South, 1895–1925. In S. Harley & R. Terborg-Penn (Eds.), *The Afro-American woman: Struggles and image* (pp. 43–57). Baltimore, MD: Black Classic.

Osborne, D. (1989, July 30). *"They can't stop us now" Kimi Gray and other residents of D.C's Kenilworth-Parkside complex have overcome poverty, crime, drugs and innumerable layers of public housing bureaucracy—not to mention charges that they're just cogs in Jack Kemp's propaganda machine. Their goal? To take control of their own lives.* Retrieved from http://pqasb.pqarchiver.com/washingtonpost/results.html?st=basic&uid=MAC=50a23aa1f3f5c6104e90e36051420d61&QryTxt=they+can%27t+stop+us+now+Kimi+Gray&sortby=RELEVANCE

Perkins, D., & Zimmerman, M. A. (1995). Empowerment theory, research, and application. *American Journal of Community Psychology, 23*, 569–599.

Perry, T. (2003). Up from the parched earth: Towards a theory of African-American achievement. In T. Perry, C. Steele, & A. G. Hilliard III, (Eds.), *Young, gifted, and Black: Promoting high achievement among African-American students* (pp. 1–108). Boston, MA: Beacon.

Perry, T., Steele, C., & Hilliard, A. G. III. (2003). *Young, gifted, and Black: Promoting high achievement among African-American students.* Boston, MA: Beacon.

Pianta, R. C., & Walsh, D. J. (1998). Applying the construct of resilience in schools: Cautions from a developmental systems perspective. *School Psychology Review, 27*, 407–417.

Pollitzer, W. S. (1999). *The Gullah people and their African heritage.* Athens: University of Georgia Press.

Promising Practices Network. (2013). *Child-parent centers.* Retrieved from http://www.promisingpractices.net/program.asp?programid=98

Property Nut. (2011). *Romantic plantation home* [Real estate listing]. Retrieved June 27, 2012, from http://www.propertynut.com/listings/Georgia/Locust%20Grove/-Romantic-Plantation-Home/26546

Putnam, R. D. (1995). Tuning in, tuning out: The strange disappearance of social capital in America. *PS: Political Science & Politics, 28*, 664–683.

Rainer, V. T. (1971). *Henry county Georgia: The mother of counties.* McDonough, GA.

Randall, D. (1969). *Booker T. and W. E. B.* Retrieved from http://www.poetryfoundation.org/poem/177161

Rappaport, J. (2000). Community narratives: Tales of terror and joy. *American Journal of Community Psychology, 28*, 1–24.

Robinson, F. P. (2000). *Is urban education too hard for God?* Fort Washington, MD: Silesia.

Robinson, R. (1999). *Defending the spirit: A Black life in America.* New York, NY: Penguin.

Rogers, S. H., Halstead, J. M., Gardner, K. H., & Carlson, C. H. (2011). Examining walkability and social capital as indicators of quality of life at the municipal and neighborhood scale. *Applied Research in Quality of Life, 6*(2), 201–213.

Rogoff, B., Paradise, R., Arauz, R. M., Correa-Chavez, M., & Angelillo, C. (2003). Firsthand learning through intent participation. *Annual Review of Psychology, 54,* 175–203.

Roots. (1999, November). *City Beat,* p. 3. Atlanta, GA: City of Atlanta.

Rouse, J. A. (1995). Introduction. In Robert W. Woodruff Library, Atlanta University Center, *The Neighborhood Union Collection (1908–1961).* Retrieved from http://www.auctr.edu/rwwl/FindingAids%5CNeighborhood%20 Union%20Collection.pdf

Rury, J. (2004). *Education and social change: Themes in the history of American schooling.* Mahway, NJ: Lawrence Erlbaum.

Rutter, M. (1987). Psychosocial resilience and protective mechanisms. *American Journal of Orthopsychiatry, 57,* 316–331.

Rymer, R. (1998). *American beach: How "progress" robbed a Black town—and nation—of history, wealth, and power.* New York, NY: HarperPerennial.

Sanders, M. G. (2006). *Building school-community partnerships: Collaboration for student success.* Thousand Oaks, CA: Corwin.

Sanders, M. G., & Sheldon, S. B. (2009). *Principals matter: A guide to school, family, and community partnerships.* Thousand Oaks, CA: Corwin.

Schomburg Center for Research in Black Culture. (2000). *The Black New Yorkers: The Schomburg illustrated chronology.* New York, NY: John Wiley & Sons.

Schutz, A. (1997). *The metaphor of "space" in educational theory: Henry Giroux through the eyes of Hannah Arendt and Michel Foucault.* Retrieved from http://ojs.ed.uiuc.edu/index.php/pes/article/viewArticle/2793

Scout promotions won by Scott, Westmoreland. (1933, November 27). *Atlanta Daily World,* p. 1. Retrieved from www.proquest.com/en-US/catalogs/databases/detail/histnews-bn.shtml

Several local boy scouts are given special recognition at first court of honor. (1936, January 29). *Atlanta Daily World,* p. 1. Retrieved from www.proquest.com/en-US/catalog/databases/detail/histnews-bn.shtml

Shade, B. J., Kelly, C., & Oberg, M. (1997). *Creating culturally responsive classrooms.* Washington, DC: American Psychological Association.

Simons, L. M. (1978, August 6). Unique group gets youths into college. *Washington Post.* Retrieved July 31, 2003, http://pqasb.pqarchiver.com/washingtonpost_historical/results.html?st=basic&uid=&MAC=50a23aa1f3f5c6 104e90e36051420d61&QryTxt=unique+group+gets+youths+in+college& sortby=RELEVANCE&restrict=articles

Sobel, D. (2002). *Children's special places: Exploring the role of forts, dens, and bush houses in middle childhood.* Detroit, MI: Wayne State University Press.

Southern Education Foundation. (2010). *A new diverse minority: Students of color in the South's public schools.* Atlanta, GA: Author. Retrieved from www.southerneducation.org

Stack, C. (1996). *Call to home: African Americans reclaim the rural South.* New York: Basic.

Stanton Elementary School. (1996). *Title 1 local school improvement plan, 1996–1997.* Washington, DC: Author.

Stanton Elementary School. (1997). *Local school integrated improvement plan, up-date 1997–1998*. Washington, DC: Author.

Sutton, S. E. (1996). *Weaving a tapestry of resistance: The places, power, and poetry of a sustainable society*. Westport, CT: Bergin & Garvey.

Sutton, S. E., & Kemp, S. P. (2006). Young people's participation in constructing a socially just public sphere. In C. Spencer & M. Blades (Eds.), *Children and their environments: Learning, using, and designing spaces* (pp. 256–275). New York, NY: Cambridge University Press.

Swanson, D. P., Cunningham, M., Youngblood, J., & Spencer, M. B. (2009). *Racial identity development during childhood*. In H. A. Neville, B. M. Tynes, & S. O. Utsey (Eds.), *Handbook of African American psychology* (pp. 269–281). Thousand Oaks, CA: Sage.

Swimming upstream. (1999, November). *City Beat*, p. 1. Atlanta, GA: City of Atlanta.

Taylor, A. F., Wiley, A., & Kuo, F. E. (1998). Growing up in the inner city: Green spaces as places to grow. *Environment and Behavior, 30*, 3–27.

Trickett, E. J., & Moos, R. H. (1973). Social environment of junior high school and high school classrooms. *Journal of Educational Psychology, 65*, 93–102.

Trickett, E. J., & Todd, D. M. (1972). The high school culture: An ecological perspective. *Theory into Practice, 11*, 8–37.

Trumbull, E., Rothstein-Fisch, C., Greenfield, P. M., & Quiroz, B. (2001). *Bridging cultures between home and school: A guide for teachers*. Mahway, NJ: Lawrence Erlbaum.

Tuan, Y. (1977). *Space and place: The perspective of experience*. Minneapolis: University of Minnesota Press.

Tucker, C. M., & Herman, K. C. (2002). Using culturally sensitive theories and research to meet the academic needs of low-income African American children. *American Psychologist, 57*, 762–773.

Turner, E. H. (2000). The education of Jacob Lawrence. In P. T. Nesbett & M. DuBois (Eds.), *Over the line: The art and life of Jacob Lawrence* (pp. 97–109). Seattle: University of Washington Press.

Turner, F. R. (Compiler). (1995). *1870 census Henry County, Georgia*. Atlanta, GA: The R. J. Taylor, Jr., Foundation.

U.S. Census Bureau. *Public Education Finances: 2010, G10-ASPEF*. Washington, DC: U.S. Government Printing Office.

Washington, B. T. (1901). *Up from slavery: An autobiography*. Retrieved from http://docsouth.unc.edu/fpn/washington/menu.html

Washington, B. T. (1895). Booker T. Washington delivers the 1895 Atlanta Compromise speech. *History Matters*. Retrieved from http://historymatters.gmu.edu/d/39/

Washington Park—A history. (1999, November). *City Beat, 2*, 2.

Webber, T. L. (1978). *Deep like the rivers: Education in the slave quarter community, 1831–1865*. New York, NY: W.W. Norton.

Wentzel, K. R. (1999). Social influences on school adjustment: Commentary. *Educational Psychologist, 34*(1), 59–69.

Westmacott, R. (1992). *African-American gardens and yards in the rural south.* Knoxville: University of Tennessee Press.

Wight, V. R., Chau, M., & Aratani, Y. (2011). Who are America's poor children? The official story. *National Center for Children in Poverty.* Retrieved from http://www.nccp.org/publications/pdf/text_958.pdf

Williams, H. A. (2005). *Self-taught: African American education in slavery and freedom.* Chapel Hill: University of North Carolina Press.

Willis, D. (2000). *Reflections in Black: A history of Black photographers 1840 to the present.* New York, NY: W. W. Norton.

Wilson, W. J. (1987). *The truly disadvantaged: The inner city, the underclass, and public policy.* Chicago, IL: University of Chicago Press.

Woolley, M., Grogan-Kaylor, A., Gilster, M. E., Karb. R. A., Gant, L. M., Reischl, T. M., & Alaimo, K. (2008). Neighborhood social capital, poor physical conditions, and school achievement. *Children & Schools, 30,* 133–145.

Wright, R. (2005). *Black boy (American hunger: A record of childhood and youth).* New York, NY: HarperCollins.